BEHIND THE BADGE

R. J. Bonett

Copyright © 2024 by R. J. Bonett

Behind the Badge

All rights reserved.

No part of this publication may be reproduced or transmitted in any form or by any means electronic or mechanical, including photocopy, recording, or any information storage and retrieval system now known or invented, without permission in writing from the publisher, except by a reviewer who wishes to quote brief passages in connection with a review written for inclusion in a magazine, newspaper, or broadcast.

Disclaimer:
Although this work is true, the similarity to real names
of the characters is coincidental.

Credits:
Editor: Rachel Heitzenrater

Special thanks to several people: The book title, *Behind the Badge* was a suggestion by a close friend, Ann Marie Danvers.

The manuscript was reviewed for its content
by a close friend and avid reader, Patricia Ziegler.

The cover design was put together by R. J. Bonett, with the help and expertise of Karen DeLise from New York Camera & Video, 1139 Street Road Southampton, Pennsylvania 18966. The wording on the front cover was done by Todd Heckler of Wellsboro, Pa.

Also: a special mention to a friend Jerry Rocks Sr.
or the photo of the police wagon in the background.

Print ISBN: 979-8-35092-947-8
eBook ISBN: 979-8-35092-948-5

Printed in the United States of America

This is one man's story of the times and experiences while a member of the police department in the city of Philadelphia, between the years 1967 and 1989.

In those days a police officer's job was completely different than it is today. Randy Bishop reflects on his years as a cop and takes readers on a journey more than 50 years ago in urban Philly, where crime was rampant and the criminals unforgiving. While telling a tale of growing his police career, he also shares happy moments of being on the force- as well as sad- and gives readers a lesson on what it truly meant to be a police officer in one of America's most dangerous cities. Readers will envelope themselves into stories about investigating homicides, serving drug warrants, court-room procedures and the brotherhood of "Backing the badge."

Although the names of the characters are altered, the situations are exactly as reported, some good, some bad, some humorous, but all factual.

I realize there are certain people who may take offense to what they read, but the point is to expose those experiences as lived. I sincerely hope you enjoy the read.

TABLE OF CONTENTS

CHAPTER 1.	*Joining the Department*	1
CHAPTER 2.	*Transferred*	9
CHAPTER 3.	*Being assigned*	26
CHAPTER 4.	*Working a district*	32
CHAPTER 5.	*Two Squad*	41
CHAPTER 6.	*The J/R*	49
CHAPTER 7.	*Jesse*	53
CHAPTER 8.	*Warrants*	62
CHAPTER 9.	*The Muslims*	71
CHAPTER 10.	*Drug distribution*	78
CHAPTER 11.	*Reshuffling the deck*	86
CHAPTER 12.	*Youths*	93
CHAPTER 13.	*Pet peeves*	100
CHAPTER 14.	*Domestic disturbances*	106
CHAPTER 15.	*Premonitions*	113
CHAPTER 16.	*Humorous assignments*	117
CHAPTER 17.	*Detectives*	127
CHAPTER 18.	*The Burglary Detail*	130
CHAPTER 19.	*Holiday spirit*	137
CHAPTER 20.	*Chief Surgeon Detail*	142
CHAPTER 21.	*Reuniting*	145
CHAPTER 22.	*Routine Patrol*	152
CHAPTER 23.	*Time for a change*	158
CHAPTER 24.	*Mean Gene*	173
CHAPTER 25.	*Commendations*	181
CHAPTER 26.	*Regrets*	186
EPILOGUE		189

CHAPTER 1

Joining the Department

I never gave much thought about being a cop; it was a decision more or less made by accident. I left the Marine Corps as a Sergeant in February of 1967, and was looking forward to resuming the life I had prior to my military obligation. I took a job as a draftsman at the Budd Company Railcar Division, on Red Lion Road in the Northeast section of Philadelphia. After several threats of going out on strike from union grievances with the shop-end of the company, I was getting frustrated. I had rent to pay and other financial responsibilities and couldn't afford the loss of a pay check. At the end of April I decided I had enough, and was going to return to the Marine Corps. While riding in a subway-car towards 30th Street Railroad Station, I looked up at a marquee advertising jobs with the Philadelphia Police Department. Thinking about it for a moment I figured, *Why not? I had nothing to lose."* Getting off the subway at city hall I went up the stairs and entered the building. I inquired at the information desk about the job, and was handed a 3" x 5" card to fill-out. Handing the card back, the person behind the desk noted I had just left the military and handed me a test booklet. I sat back down and answered the questions the best I could. They were general information questions about my background and education level. It also had questions pertaining to the geography of the city. After handing the test back, I was told I'd receive a card in the mail of when and where I was to go.

Within a few days the card came with the test score. I scored high, and on the card it gave the location where I was to report, the Police Administration Building at 8th and Race Street in center city. Gathering with other applicants in the auditorium on a Thursday afternoon at 4:30 p.m., we were given a lecture about the department. After the lecture, we were told to report to the Police Academy on State Road on Monday morning the 15th of May.

* * *

After arriving at the academy we were separated into two groups; around thirty people to a class. The training wasn't much physically, especially just after leaving the Marine Corps, and the introduction to the Pennsylvania Penal Code was brief. The pistol range, first aid and driving test seemed to be the highlight of our brief training, and after six weeks we graduated and given our assignments. At the time there was civil unrest in many cities and although Philadelphia was relatively calm, there were around thirty five veteran officers a month either quitting or retiring. I believe part of the reason was the twelve hour shifts we were on with no days off. At the time, the city didn't pay overtime; it was what they called compensatory time. Something you could take at a later date that somehow disappeared.

Most of the graduating -class, were detailed as a standby unit at the Palestra Stadium in West Philadelphia. The city had several busses used for transporting us in mass to any location where any civil unrest was arising.

This program was financed by the Federal Government, and with that knowledge, I realized it wouldn't go away anytime soon.

As the shortage of men continued, a few of us were sent to a taskforce unit. This was a separate unit that would normally work from 7 p.m. to 3 a.m., overlapping the normal squads in districts. The assignments were always in the busier districts with the highest crime rate.

Being one of the men assigned to task force, I didn't care for the hours. It was mid-summer and we had been on a schedule of twelve hour days with no days off since graduating from the Police Academy. I had been working with several different people there, but realized at some point, I would be assigned a permanent partner. Several weeks after Labor Day, the twelve hour shifts ended, and I was told I would be working with a veteran cop by the nickname of Iron Mike.

* * *

The day I was to be assigned, I left my apartment wondering what the new partner would be like, and walking to my car, I looked up at the unusually brisk late afternoon September sky. Fall was in the air, and I was hoping cooler temperatures would have an effect on whether the radio calls would be light or heavy for the 7 p.m. to 3 a.m. shift. Fridays were always busy in police work, but I was hoping cooler temperatures would prevail.

After arriving at headquarters, I could hear the crackle of police broadcasts from some of the districts in the operations room, and quickly realized my assumption of cooler weather having a positive affect was dead wrong. It sounded like Dodge City in the 22nd and 23rd Districts in North Philadelphia, and the same in West Division the 16th and the 18th. The West end of the 25th District sounded busy as well, and areas in South Philly were also humming with activity.

At the time, the police department in Philadelphia had three normal rotating shifts in the districts. The shifts actually worked in reverse, midnight to 8 a.m., 4 p.m., midnight, and finally 8 a.m., to 4 p.m. each weekly tour being six days in length, with two days off. Sometime later, the Fraternal Order of Police noticed we were working an extra day without pay, and instead of paying for the extra day, the city worked out a deal where we were given a day off during the month in lieu of the money.

Task Force wasn't a district per se'. We would get our assignments from a central command that kept track of high crime areas in districts we covered. The reason for the 7 p.m. to 3 a.m. hours, we were an overlapping force while the normal squads changed shifts. That, and the fact the districts we patrolled desperately needed the extra coverage.

It wasn't abnormal for the police cars permanently assigned to one of those districts to handle eighteen to twenty radio assignments on the 4p.m. to midnight tour, especially in the summer months. To give you an idea of what it was like. While working one Friday 4 p.m. to midnight in North Central, amongst other calls, there were eight shootings within an eight hour shift, four within a fifteen-minute time span. Police radio broadcaster that evening was even temporarily confused asking what cars were going in on which assignment.

We used to refer to those districts as the, *"The Wild, Wild West."* It wasn't difficult to make a gun arrest or narcotics bust in those districts, the areas were rife with that sort of activity. At times, it seemed like some of the people were oblivious to police presence, or didn't care much about punishment if caught.

I recall an incident while we were stopped in traffic on Market Street in West Philadelphia, in the 18th District. Two men walking down Market Street at 7:30 p.m., picked up a trash can and hurled it through the front window of a furniture store still open for business. Picking up a sofa, they proceeded to walk away as if it was normal, with onlookers seemingly paying little or no attention to it.

Most warm evenings were brutal, especially when the weather was hotter than normal. Oftentimes, people were still out partying at 3 or 4 a.m. I would recall many times what one veteran cop told me not long after joining the force, *"Kid, you'll find out the best cop on the street is bad weather. It keeps everybody indoors."*

I stood roll call with other members of the squad that day and we were given our assignments. The sergeant said, "Bishop, you'll be working with Iron Mike." I didn't know him personally, but already knew his reputation from other comments I had heard from other cops. Looking down the line of men I saw him looking back at me, and wondered what was going through his mind.

After roll-call we walked outside to our patrol car. After checking it for any unclaimed damage, we refueled. I was about to get in the passenger seat when he said, "Here kid," tossing me the car-keys over the hood of the car. After getting in the driver's seat he gave me a cold stare for a few moments, and I realized he was doing it for one purpose. That was to make sure he had my full attention; because what he had to say was important. Sensing I was becoming uncomfortable, he finally said, "Remember this kid, it's better to be tried by twelve than carried by six. Now drive and don't get me fucking killed."

I realized the power of that statement within the first two hours of the shift. Driving east on Indiana Avenue, around 6th Street, there was a guy holding a shotgun on another male. Mike quickly said, "Pin him to the wall." Without hesitation I drove up on the sidewalk as he commanded, and quickly exited the vehicle with my service revolver at the ready. I believe I impressed him with that first encounter and we fell into a mutual trust of having one another's back.

I enjoyed driving and I believe it gave Mike the ability to observe more around us, something that would become second nature after being on the street for awhile. One of his strongest points was having a knack for sensing stolen cars. The same night as the shotgun incident, we were traveling west along Lehigh Avenue. The street's wide enough to handle a parking lane on each side and two traffic lanes in each direction. Around 8th Street, he observed a car load of what appeared to be Hispanic kids driving east. I never noticed them but Mike said, "Make a U-turn and get behind that green Chevy." I did as I was told and within a few blocks caught up to the car. Looking at the hot sheet, (*a paper printed daily with stolen auto license plate numbers*) he said, "That's a stolen car, give him the lights."

I was amazed at his perception of being able to sense things like that, and within the first month of working together we recovered around 20 stolen auto's 12 with occupants.

* * *

After six months of working with Mike, I walked into the district one Friday night and stood roll-call with other members of the squad. When the assigned districts were given, my name wasn't called and when we were dismissed, I asked,

"Sergeant, you didn't give me an assignment."

"See the Corporal in the operations -room, he has a teletype message for you."

"What's it about?"

Nonchalantly replying as he looked at his clip-board, "I don't really know. I think you're being transferred, go check it out."

Entering the operations room I asked, "Hey Corporal, the sergeant told me you wanted to see me."

"Yeah, you've been transferred to the 15th." pausing for a moment he looked up from adjusting paperwork on his desk and said, "You lucky dog. Go home and report in at 9 a.m. on Monday," pausing again from putting a clipboard back on its hanger he asked, "By the way, who do you know?"

"It's as much as a surprise to me as it is to you. Anyway, who'll be working with Iron Mike?"

"Don't worry. I'll get him a replacement."

"Make sure whoever it is can keep the pace. Mike's still a go getter."

"Yeah, I know. You two made a great team."

Walking out of the building, I saw Mike coming toward me. "Mike, I'm being…" I didn't have time to complete the sentence when he said "I just heard. I want to know who I'll be working with," as he hurried by me heading for the door of the district I said, "I think it's McCloskey, but I'm not sure. Whoever it is, make sure he has your back."

Turning to me before entering the building he said, "That's what I want to make sure of. It's been great working with you Bishop. Take care and remember what I told you when we first hit the street. Even though you're going to a quieter district, it only takes one asshole to take your life."

After shaking hands I got in my vehicle and pulled out of the parking lot.

Mike was my mentor for the last few months and driving home, my mind drifted back to the first time we met. Mike was in his late forties, a Korean War Vet, and in tremendous shape for his age. With a head full of gray hair, he stood around six feet tall and looked distinguished in uniform. I think we hit it off from the start by both being ex-Marines and although I was never certain, the title Iron Mike probably came from the statue out in front of Marine Corps Headquarters on Parris Island. It was the statue of a muscular WWI Marine holding a machine gun over one shoulder.

Driving home I thought the Corporals statement was right. *We did make a great team.* We averaged several gun arrests amongst other felonies per month. I realized Mike was essential for another reason. Due to the lack of personnel, our class only spent 6 weeks in the Police Academy. It was him who actually taught me what we call street smarts, and because of Mike, I felt like I was prepared to be a part of any police district, and wondered what the 15th was going to be like.

CHAPTER 2

Transferred

Not being familiar with the 15th, I spent part of the weekend traveling the district to become familiar with it. True, my apartment was in that end of the city, but aside from that, I never had the need to be there.

I was born and raised in the Tioga section of North Philadelphia, and knew quite a bit about it, especially the 39th, district located at 22nd and Hunting Park, the district that covers the Tioga section. I was also pretty familiar with the west end of the 25th, and the north end of the 22nd. That too, aided Mike and I with our success. The main thoroughfare through the 15th was the Roosevelt Boulevard. There are three center lanes in each direction with narrow grass separations and three outer lanes with one parking lane for turns off the main corridor. It's actually Route 1 through the city. Frankford Avenue is another main artery running north and south through the district. It's actually Route 13 and historically called The Kings Highway. It was said that George Washington and his army traversed that highway in route to the battle of Trenton. Aramingo Avenue is another and although it's not a numbered state route, it accommodated most of the traffic from center city before Route 95 was built. For some unknown reason, the name changes to Harbison Avenue at Torresdale, and Harbison Avenue and Levick Street is where the 15th District is located. The building is actually headquarters for the 15th; the 2nd District and North East Detective Division.

Until being transferred, I only had the occasion to be in the building once. While assigned to taskforce, I had to take my police vehicle to the radio repair shop which was located at the police academy in the Northeast at that time. The radio could receive calls but couldn't transmit.

While in slow moving traffic on the way there, there was a radio broadcast of a holdup of a gas station in the Torresdale section of the 15th. To my surprise, I noticed the vehicle directly in front of me was the vehicle described in the broadcast bearing the same license plate number. There were three occupants and I blew the horn signaling the driver to pull over. Instead, he drove over the small grass island separating the northbound lanes, and I was forced to follow.

Other drivers saw what was taking place, and cars began to fall behind us allowing me to maneuver to the left side of the car. The driver began nudging my vehicle with his, trying to force me back onto the small island to make contact with one of several trees, and after striking my vehicle a few times, I decided to take a shot at striking his left front fender forcing him to a stop. The vehicles were locked together and I quickly exited the car and went over the hood of my vehicle and the hood of the suspect's auto.

The passenger in the rear seat ran, but I had to struggle with the driver and the person in the passenger side front seat. I assumed someone in one of the houses along the boulevard must have called an assist officer, and within several minutes two police cars and a police wagon were on the scene. Calling to mind what happened that day I thought, *"If the men I have to work with in the 15th are as efficient as they were that day, there wouldn't be a problem with being backed up."*

BEHIND THE BADGE

* * *

Several days later, I received a court notice for the preliminary hearing in the district for that arrest. The case against the perpetrators of the holdup was robbery, stolen auto, and damage to city property. It was also my first introduction to something I never expected. The preliminary hearings took place in a community room or what we called the "roll room." It's where we line up for inspection to receive orders from the sergeant or lieutenant before hitting the street. As I was coming into the building, the main defendant was coming down the hall with who I suspected was his father or another relative that had his arm around the defendant's shoulder. As they passed, I heard the person with his hand around the defendants neck say, "You stupid ass, you know what you just cost me?"

Surprised he was exiting the building, I reported to the Assistant District Attorney's desk. The courtroom was busy and I stood waiting to be acknowledged. In a few minutes the Assistant D.A. read my court notice, signed it, and handed it back to me excusing me from the case.

I said, "I just saw the defendant leave the building. Is he waiving the preliminary hearing?" which was his right, if he wanted to go directly to trial in Common Pleas Court located in City Hall at that time.

Instead, the District Attorney looked up at me and said, "The case has been adjudicated." I left the room baffled as to why, but several months later, after being transferred to the 15th I realized the connection. His father owned one of the largest auto body and fender businesses in the city. He probably influenced the outcome monetarily with the gas station, and whoever was behind correcting the damage to city property, which more than likely was his company.

At the time, there was what we called ambulance chasers. The father had a police receiver in his office, and when a broadcast of an auto accident was heard anywhere in the northeast, he would send someone to the scene to solicit the owners of the vehicles for the repair work, a practice that was illegal in the city.

As a cop assigned to the accident, you were supposed to tell them to leave the scene, and warn the owners of the vehicles involved in the accident of the possibility of a higher than normal price for the repair. Depending on the extent of the damage, the price would be jacked up to cover the deductable and a little extra for the owner of the vehicle. There was also a gratuity to the cop for allowing it to happen, but in time with younger cops being assigned to the district and insurance companies more closely reviewing repair work; that practice faded away.

After familiarizing myself with the main arteries of the district and a few of the larger streets, I went home.

* * *

Monday morning at 9 a.m., as instructed, I reported in. There were several other cops I went through the Police Academy with and we waited in the captain's office for him to arrive. Captain Maloney entered the room around 9:15 and introduced himself. He was an older man probably in his mid to late fifties. It was hard to tell, he could have passed for W.C. Fields' red nose and all. After looking at the sheet with our names and addresses he said, "I see you're all residents of the northeast, I guess you're familiar with the district."

I thought, *"That statement couldn't be farther from the truth. If I hadn't driven around the district over the weekend, I probably wouldn't have been able to find the police station."*

I and another cop by the name of Bob Charles were assigned to two-squad. They were on day work and we waited for the sergeant to assign us to whatever end of the district we were needed. The squads were broken into A and B Platoon so at the change of shift, A squad with even numbered cars would report off on the hour, and B platoon the odd numbered cars would report off on the half hour. That way there would be constant coverage on the street.

I was assigned the lower end of the district known as Frankford, Bridesburg, and the Northwood section. Bob was assigned the upper end or what they called the Wissinoming, Mayfair, Tacony and Torresdale section of the city.

At that time the 15th was one of the larger districts. It was mainly comprised of upper and middleclass residents in the northern section, and west of Frankford Avenue in the lower end. The east side of Frankford was middle to lower income families with a public housing project. To the extreme east an area known as the Bridesburg section, was primarily made up of working class Polish and Ukrainian people.

Some of the sectors in the 15th were half the size of an entire district in North Philadelphia or West Philadelphia. Within a few years after being assigned, the loss of economics would bring about a drastic change in sector size. The highest number police car when I arrived was 1518, and by the time I retired, the highest number police car was 1522. From what I understand, today the highest car number is somewhere in the thirty range.

The Sergeant, Bill Jackson, finally arrived and assigned Bob to a police car in the Mayfair section with a veteran officer, and told me to wait for the lower end sergeant to give me my assignment. After about twenty minutes, Sergeant Ruff came into the district. After a few words with the Corporal, he had me follow him to his vehicle. He was around five feet ten, bald and on the portly side. I remember looking at his profile as I got in the passenger seat thinking, *"He looks like the profile of Alfred Hitchcock in the television series."*

He spoke with a hurried tone and rattled off questions as to where and what my background was in the police department.

Having a hard time keeping pace with his questions, he finally subsided asking, "Are you familiar with the district?"

After telling him the truth that I wasn't, he said, "I'll give you a little tour to familiarize you with some of it."

He drove around for the better part of two hours filling me in on different neighborhoods, and as we were riding through the Bridesburg section he said, "Notice the smell? This area is like driving through a gigantic fart. Several chemical companies and a variety of other industrial manufacturers make up that smell." He was of course correct, and in time that too would change with the loss of industry.

After the tour, he dropped me off at a school crossing at Penn and Orthodox Streets and said, "There is one thing I'd like to say about working a district like this. The job is about 98% boring and about 2% sheer terror. I'll be back after the school crossing."

He never said whether it was the afternoon or final dismissal and I waited until 3:45 for him to return. With his nervous demeanor I realized he probably forgot me, and I decided to walk two blocks to Frankford Avenue, a business strip through the entire lower end.

I hopped a bus which ended its run at the Bridge Street Terminal, a major transit hub and the last stop of the elevated train from center city. Standing at Bridge Street, I looked to see if I could possibly flag a police car heading for the district. I didn't see one, but while standing there, a private vehicle pulled up and a uniformed cop rolled down his window and asked, "Hey kid, you going to the district?"

Quickly replying, "Yes," I got in. He looked to be in his early 60's with a full head of gray hair and sharp facial features. He identified himself as

Charlie Healey, a beat cop and the most senior member of 2 Squad. In turn I told him who I was and related the sergeant putting me on a school crossing, then forgetting me. When he laughed I thought, "*With that response, I realized I was probably correct with my assumption, it was normal for the sergeant's demeanor.*"

* * *

The next day at the first roll -call, l stood in the back of the room looking over the squad. Most of the men I assumed were in their mid -forties to early fifties, and I would discover in time, most were WWII and Korean War Veterans.

Throughout the years, like working with Mike, I learned a lot about patience that seemed to come natural to these guys. Frank Zornek, who became one of my main mentors, was wounded at the battle of Iwo Jima while stationed aboard the U.S.S. Pensacola, a heavy cruiser when the ship was struck by Japanese shore batteries.

Frank's partner Charlie Kamp fought at the Battle of The Bulge and Lou Ellinger was a paratrooper with the 101st Airborne Division. Eddie Bonk, Joe Kennedy and a few others also had colorful war records.

They were part of the generation we were replacing and frankly, I don't think they could have kept pace with societal changes. The drug culture was beginning to have an enormous effect on the increasing crime rate on our society, and I knew it would only be a matter of time before it caught up to this area.

Although they were patient when it came to dealing with stressful situations one on one, they weren't going to stand and take physical abuse because of political correctness during the civil unrest at the time.

* * *

The second day in the district I stood roll call with the other members of 2 Squad. There were several younger cops close to my age or just a little older, so I didn't feel completely out of place. After roll call, we went to our different assignments. Fortunately, I was assigned to 1500 wagon with Frank Zornek. His normal partner Charlie Kamp was off for some reason and I was temporarily replacing him.

The contrast between the districts I was used to working was astounding. There weren't many radio calls even in our end of the district, which was supposed to be the busier end. For the exception of illegal parking complaints, there were hardly any calls broadcast during the day shift. I think the total jobs we handled on the day-work shift for several days may have numbered twelve. That included several hospital cases and taking a body to the City Morgue at 11th and Wood Street, part of the duties of the police department at the time. Being assigned with a person who had many years working the lower end, it did have an advantage. It gave me the opportunity to familiarize myself with the district.

Working with a veteran officer like Frank brings up a point of on-the-job-training. The first day assigned with him on 1500 wagon, as I got in the vehicle he placed a jar of Vicks Vapo-Rub on the console. I asked, "Frank do you have a cold?"

"No! But this is an absolute necessity for working a police wagon."

I was completely baffled until the next day when we received an assignment. After arriving, we met the complainant who stated she hadn't seen her next-door neighbor for several days. After Frank asked a few questions about the neighbor's age and possible knowledge of relatives who may live in the area, the woman stated she knew the neighbor really didn't have any visitors.

Trying the front door and window to see if we could gain entry, without success, I went to the rear of the residence. The door was locked but there was a small window in the kitchen that wasn't. After opening it, I climbed in. Entering the house to unlock the front door, I immediately smelled a foul odor.

After admitting Frank he wasn't two steps into the living room when he said, "Get the jar of Vicks."

I thought, *"There's nothing like a practical lesson without speaking."*

We found the woman dead in her bedroom on the second floor. She had been there for several days, and with the warm weather, the body had already begun to decompose. The smell was rank, something you'll never forget, and even after the assignment, the odor still permeated our clothing.

The few radio assignments we received while I was working with Frank were a far cry from the twenty plus calls that police cars assigned to North Central, West Division, or the West end of East Division, would get on a 4 p.m. to midnight shift. When I mentioned it to Frank, he didn't seem surprised and had no reaction to my statement.

One positive thing about working with him, it gave me the opportunity to learn more about the various groups of people in the district, and I soon realized it was like being on a separate police department.

To give you an idea of the changes taking place between older cops and younger cops, he seemed to be indifferent about drugs and believed it was only the responsibility of the narcotic unit. While working with Frank, we had an occasion to have to transport prisoners to the district for the arresting officer. When they emptied their pockets at the counter, which was customary, I noticed two glazed packets from one of the prisoners. When Frank asked what they were, the prisoner replied, "B. C.," which was the short term for bicarbonate of soda, he claimed for upset stomachs.

With that, I shoved him against the counter and said, "Now tell him what it really is!"

Frank looked surprised at my action and asked, "What is it?"

"It's probably heroine Frank."

After resuming patrol, I related several stories of pretty substantial narcotics arrests Mike and I made, but I don't believe telling him changed his indifferent attitude, or made him aware of what was causing the rapid societal changes taking place. I felt most cops his age were still locked into the idea that real crime was burglary, robbery, auto theft and other crimes, without realizing the depth of the cancer causing it.

With three main elevated train stations and a major bus terminal in the lower end, the foot traffic was considerable but primarily without incident.

I do recall the first signs of increasing crime due to drug use. Most of the cars in the public parking lot in and around the Bridge Street train station belonged to commuters traveling by elevated train to center city. These cars began falling victim to quite a few auto thefts and car burglaries. It was a quick way for a junkie to make a score of something of value the owner may have left in plain sight, and sold for a few dollars to support a drug habit.

After several weeks of working with Frank, his partner returned and I was reassigned a foot beat.

In those days when you were assigned to a district, older cops generally kept their distance. The reason behind this behavior was not knowing whether you were placed in the squad as what they commonly referred to as ginks, people from the Internal Security Unit. That was a unit in the police department to weed out possible corruption in districts. They were like a police department for the police department.

For the first several months, most newcomers like myself, were assigned foot beats generally on the business strips in Frankford, Mayfair, or the Torresdale section. The neighborhoods hadn't yet changed and businesses didn't need to have metal gratings covering the front windows.

It was common practice for people leaving local theaters at night, or even on a Sunday after leaving church, to take a stroll along the main shopping areas to view merchandise in the windows on display. Even jewelry stores at that time kept merchandise in the windows. My first encounter in the 15th of what we called a "smash and grab" occurred on my first Easter Sunday day work in the district.

I was assigned a foot beat on the 4600 and 4700 blocks of Frankford Avenue. As I was exiting a restaurant, I observed a car pull up in front of a jewelry store on the opposite side of the street. I had a suspicion they were about to smash and grab the store, and walked across the street. The passenger exited the car and walked up to the window with what looked like a club in his hand. The driver, focusing on the person about to smash the window, never looked in my direction.

His window was open, and I attempted to reach in and grab the car keys. Surprised, he looked at me and quickly put the car in gear and began driving down the avenue. I was holding on to the vehicle with one arm and with the free hand, I was able to un-holster my weapon and point it at his head. He abruptly came to a stop and the apprehension of both males was made.

They were charged with burglary, theft, and not only assault and battery of a police officer, with the intent to do bodily harm. The driver was a pretty big person whose first name was George with a long Greek last name I couldn't guess how to spell. His cohort was an Italian named Tony DiMarko.

When the case went to Common Pleas Court, they were defended by a prominent Philadelphia law firm. The defense attorney badgered me with the same questions over and over rephrasing them differently, and when the judge didn't interject, I realized where the case was going. After they were sentenced to probation, I left the courtroom. In the hall, the lawyer met me an apologized for the grilling he put me through, and I sort of gave him a facial gesture that I was aware of what took precedent; my potential bodily harm or the influence of the union.

The driver turned out to be influential with the roofers' union Local Number 30, a strong union in and around the city. The passenger who committed the smash and grab was what we call a union goon. I was always skeptical of the union. It wielded quite a bit of power in and around the city. Whenever an independent roofer was working in the tri-state area and didn't have a Local 30 sign on their vehicle, they were always subject to a beating or vandalism of their equipment, or both. That practice also included builders who didn't hire union companies to do their work.

I was always skeptical of the union members, and suspected there was some sort of connection to organized crime but wasn't sure how.

Some years later the president of the union was shot to death at the front door of his residence by someone delivering a Christmas plant.

Several years after that, George and his cohort from the smash and grab were found shot to death in an auto, parked on a lot in the Northeast section of the city. It pretty much proved that my earlier assumption was correct. From what I understood, it had something to do with drugs and organized crime, which didn't surprise me.

Off and on I was assigned to a car, but most of the time I was primarily assigned a foot beat. They weren't bad on the day-work or 4 p.m. to midnight shift, but the midnight to 8 a.m. tour was another story. It was getting toward early November and after the businesses closed, there weren't many places to get warm. December was a different story altogether, and January and February were for the most part unbearable. Like everything else in life, you put up with it until things get better.

Several months after I was in the district, I was walking the beat on a midnight to 8 a.m. shift on Frankford Avenue, which was made up of primarily business from Adams Avenue to Bridge Street under the elevated train trestle. The Elevated train trestle is at rooftop level to the three –story buildings on both sides of the avenue, and makes the street below like a wind tunnel. It was late February and the temperature was in the low twenties, with a wind blowing down Frankford Avenue, strong enough to make discarded newspaper take flight.

Around 3:30 a.m., a police car pulled up and the veteran cop called to me. He handed me a key and said, "Here kid, this is a key to the service-room at the Church Street Station. Don't freeze your ass off out here. Make a copy when you get a chance and return mine." After rolling up his window, he continued down the street. I watched as he turned off the avenue then went up the steps to the service-room to "catch a heat," as we called it.

While sitting on the bench in the utility room getting warm, my mind drifted back to the beginning of January when I was detailed to South Philadelphia. Business owners were experiencing smashed windows and merchandise being stolen along South Street. The business association, having influence at City Hall, had the police department assign one block foot beats to cover the area, and my responsibility was between 6th and 7th Street. Another cop by the name of George Veranno was from 7th to 8th and a cop by the name of Fred Allen was from 8th to 9th.

Like tonight, the streets were ice covered and it was hard pressed to try staying warm. Around 3 a.m., for some excitement, George threw a snowball at Fred when he got to their adjoining intersection. It didn't hit him, but was probably enough to put Fred over the line as far as walking a beat where you were literally freezing to death. He waved for George and me to meet him and when we got together he said, "Hey! Fuck this," and handed me his service revolver.

Surprised, I asked, "What's the problem?"

"Look around! Do you see anyone walking the street? Hell no! They have the good sense to stay home in a warm bed. I can get a job anywhere without freezing to death," he said as he walked away. When the sergeant came around to check the detail, I handed him George's revolver and told him what George said. After signing my patrol log, he handed it back saying, "I don't blame him. This assignment really does suck."

As he drove away I thought, *"He's right. We were getting paid around $5,700 per year, when truck drivers were earning around $7,000 and jobs were plentiful in and around the city."*

I also reflected back on a similar situation of someone abruptly quitting the job. It occurred in the summer months prior to me being transferred from Task Force. In the 22nd District in North Central Division, the Raymond Rosen Public Housing Projects were at 22nd and Diamond Street. Iron Mike and I responded to a radio broadcast of a man with a gun at that location. The project was made up of several buildings, if I remember correctly, were five or six stories tall. It was normal for the police getting a call for any reason to have a second police car keep an eye on the first, while the officers were handling the assignment.

A cop by the name of Charlie Dorner was the first backup for me and Iron Mike. Charlie and I were classmates in the Police Academy. He was a burly looking kind of guy, who like me, was in his early twenties. We were the first police car at the location. While Charlie was standing outside his police car, someone threw a brick out of a window from one of the upper floors that went through the windshield of his patrol car. Fortunately, he wasn't sitting in the driver's seat. When we returned to our vehicle, he handed Mike his service revolver and me the keys to his car. He too followed that action by saying, "Tell the Sergeant to shove this job up his ass," and then walked away. I never saw him again.

If one had to judge his profession by his looks and character, putting a Jeff Cap on him and placing him behind the steering wheel of a truck would be a perfect fit. I never understood why he wanted to be a cop in the first place. He owned several trash trucks serving private businesses and from what I understood, he was pretty well off.

Suddenly, I wondered why I was reflecting back at the different situations. Was it because I was getting frustrated and in the back of my mind looking for a way out? Maybe! But there were other people I knew who left for different reasons.

Take for example, a cop I met who worked in a different squad whose name was Ojars. O, as everyone referred to him, was a tall well-built Swede who came from a well to do family. His father owned a successful contracting business building all the franchises of a fast-food chain in the tri-state area. His parents lived in a palatial home along the Delaware River between Washington's Crossing and New Hope, Pennsylvania. Instead of being a part of his father's business, he joined the police department. It could have only been for one reason, either the challenge, or like myself, just wanting to serve John Q Public.

He worked with a black officer in 158 Police Car for several years, then quit, probably by finally coming to his senses. Sometimes no matter how dedicated you are to a commitment, at times trying to do the job of a cop feels as though you're trying to shovel manure against an oncoming tide.

After reflecting, I felt warm enough to return to the beat. Walking out on the avenue, a blast of cold air quickly brought me back to reality. I was grateful for the advice and the key Lou gave me. It was certainly an act of trust and I tried to imagine why the change all of a sudden.

Lou was in his early fifties and stood slightly over six feet tall. He was bald save a patch of white hair surrounding his head. He was still in good shape for his age, and worked 156 Car for the better part of twenty five plus years. I think he knew most of the people in Frankford and I heard a few refer to him as "Pop-Pop." Like other older cops, he began to trust I wasn't a part of Internal Security sent to spy, and I believe the reason for that was an assignment he received shortly after I arrived in the district.

He was called to an assignment of an auto accident at Paul and Ruan Street, cattycorner to Monta DeLarosa Catholic Church. I was assigned to a car that evening, a quiet 4 p.m. to midnight shift, and for no other reason than the lack of activity, rode in on his assignment. The autos involved were off to the side and I exited my vehicle to see if I could assist.

There were several youths who appeared to be in their late teens or early twenties that seemed to be giving Lou a hard time. As one of them was getting out of hand, I punched him on the side of the head knocking him to the ground. That sort of settled the rest of his friends.

After picking him up I smelled alcohol on his breath, and after the occupant of the vehicle that was struck said he was the driver of the striking vehicle, I put the handcuffs on him and called for a police wagon. The driver of the vehicle struck, also told me the youths hid a case of beer on a vacant lot opposite the corner from the church after the accident, and pointed in that direction. After retrieving the liquor, I assisted Lou handling the job then resumed patrol.

The following day when I reported in for the 4 p.m. to midnight shift, after roll-call, the sergeant approached me and asked, "Did you punch someone who was involved in an accident across from the church at Paul and Ruan Street yesterday?"

"Yes! Why?"

"There was a priest watching from the Church Rectory across the street. He saw what went on and wants to see you."

"Do you know why?"

"No! But Father Palumbo is an important member of that community. He's also the Cavaliere of the Sons of Italy for Pennsylvania, the highest rank you can attain. He's also a close friend of the Deputy Commissioner," who, at the time I might add, was Frank Rizzo.

For a moment driving to the rectory, I envisioned my transfer to the 15th being short-lived, and wasn't looking forward to going back to Task Force or any other district.

After arriving at the rectory, I knocked at the door and a short distinguished gentleman in his late 50's answered. He was wearing a T-shirt and identified himself as Father Palumbo, the head priest of the Parish. I was about to put up a defense when he interrupted me saying, "The driver of the auto that was struck is a priest from this parish. I'm glad you came to backup Lou. He's getting kind of old to be tussling with young kids. What you did is more of what's needed."

After asking my name and a brief conversation, I left. What I thought was going to be an admonishment was anything but, and I felt secure I wasn't going to be transferred.

I learned later that Lou was the acting sergeant of the squad in the early fifties, and although I never knew for sure, I believe it was through his influence, I was given a permanent assignment.

CHAPTER 3

Being assigned

After almost a year in the district, in early fall of 1969 the dream of a steady car became a reality, I was assigned police car 157. At first I wasn't really sure if it was a good move or punishment. The car was a 1965 Ford with what we called a "gumball machine" on the roof. It was also probably the last stick-shift automobile in the police department.

The first night of the 4 p.m. to midnight shift, I took the back streets to Frankford Avenue and swung south heading for my sector. In traffic, I got behind a thirty-two-foot straight job truck, with the length, indicating the cargo space; I noticed the license plate was hanging. Another thing Mike taught me was to look at the driver's side mirror of the vehicle you're following. If the driver seems more interested in what you're doing, chances are something's wrong.

With the license plate hanging and the driver's primary interest in watching me, I radio checked the license tag number. After a few moments, the radio dispatcher said the truck was reported stolen from a company in Lancaster, Pennsylvania. I gave radio my location then signaled the truck driver to pull over, which he did without hesitation. The driver and passenger exited the vehicle and within minutes, 1503 police wagon pulled up behind me. Its area of responsibility was Mayfair but just happened to be leaving the district. The driver was a cop named Joe Franks and his partner was Dick Arlee. Upon investigating the cargo space, the truck seemed to be fully loaded with stolen goods. After placing the driver and passenger in the wagon, Policeman Arlee drove the truck to the district with me following.

It was also one of several questionable encounters I wasn't familiar with in other districts.

After making the initial report, the corporal never sent the job upstairs to Northeast Detective Division, and I was never asked to sign the affiant paperwork for the arrest.

In all honesty, giving the distance where the truck was stolen, it may have been because the owner didn't want to get involved more than getting his goods returned. If that was the case, I'm sure there was a gratuitous exchange of some sort.

There was another memorable incident I can recall to mind that seemed dubious. It occurred not long after I came to the district. For some reason Jesse Strange's usual partner was off that 4 p.m. to midnight shift and I was assigned with him. Around 8 p.m. we responded to a radio call to meet the complainant. After arriving, the complainant said he hadn't seen his neighbor for several days. He further stated the neighbor was an old man who had no relatives that he was aware of.

After trying the front and back doors and windows without success, I asked the neighbor if I could use his house to get to the porch roof and see if the upstairs window could be open. Fortunately, the window wasn't locked and I entered the house. After turning on the light, just as I expected, I saw the occupant lying on the bedroom floor, obviously dead. It was hard to tell how long he'd been lying there; the color of his skin was a deep blue.

After going downstairs, I removed a pile of mail from in front of the front door, and opened it to allow Jesse to come in. The neighbor also stepped into the house and after a few more questions about anyone possibly living nearby we could contact, he repeated he didn't know of anyone then left the house, probably due to the foul odor.

The place was a mess. I remembered seeing the old man walking the streets on trash night pushing a grocery cart picking through trash for anything of value. The home was as one would expect of that sort of person, it seemed he kept most of what he found throughout the downstairs. There were piles of old magazines and stacks of newspapers lying about, and the dust on the few pieces of furniture indicated they hadn't been wiped clean for ages.

I was able to get his name by looking at the mail I picked up by the front door then looked around for a telephone. There was a phone-nook with a personal directory so I scanned a few pages for anyone with the same last name, or a name with an address nearby. There were only a few pages with names that had pencil marks through them, probably indicating they were no longer in use for one reason or another. There was one name, however, that was the same with junior written after it. The address was in California with a phone number, so I called and a male voice answered. I asked if he was a relative of the deceased and he identified himself as his son. After informing him of the situation, I asked if there was anyone close by he wanted us to contact. He stated he was the only living relative and didn't sound very concerned. When I asked if he had an undertaker he wanted us to contact, his answer shocked me. He said annoyingly, "I don't give a damn what you do with him. Just don't bother me anymore," then slammed down the phone.

Jesse was standing there listening to the conversation and asked, "What did he say?" After repeating the words he said, "You better come here and look at this."

Following him into the dining room, I observed a stack of money on the table half wrapped in what looked like freezer paper. The stack of money measured around two feet by two feet, and around six inches high. The bills appeared to be in different denominations. There was other money in smaller stacks lying next to the bundle, probably with the intention to add them before tying the bundle together with a ball if string. Recognizing the wrap being freezer paper, I decided to go to the kitchen and open the freezer door. It too was stuffed to capacity with the same kind of bundle. After returning to the dining room, we looked in the drawers of a buffet table and found more money that wasn't wrapped.

We couldn't imagine a person would live in those conditions, and pack-rat such a horde. It was obviously insanity of some sort.

After looking at one another Jesse said, "We better call for the sergeant."

Upon his arrival, he surveyed the situation and had us call for a police wagon. After the wagon arrived we were told we did a great job, and with a pat on the back we were told to resume patrol.

Several weeks later the sergeant drove into the district with a brand new Buick. Although the sergeant was single and lived at home with his mother, I always wondered whether it was coincidental.

Getting back to my sector, I signed the few security logs of the stores that were still open. I wasn't able to sign them all, as my sector was around half the size of the 22nd or 23rd Districts in North Philadelphia, and some of the areas in West Division the 16th, and the 18th.

The sector of responsibility from East to West was Frankford Avenue to the Roosevelt Blvd., eight blocks wide. Cheltenham Avenue was the Northern boundary and Arrott Street was the southern, some eight blocks long.

There were three banks, five drug stores, three loan offices, and seven grocery stores in my area of responsibility, each having a police log that had to be signed at least once a tour. There was also an elementary school which required a school crossing post-morning, afternoon, and dismissal on the 8 a.m. to 4 p.m. shift, if there was a school crossing guard absent. All part of the sector's responsibility. That, plus handling any radio calls kept you pretty busy.

I was active as any rookie could be, and being assigned the sector car that covers the transit parking lot, I would park on a hill inside the cemetery across the street. With a pair of binoculars, I was able to view most of the parking lot without being seen, and was able to make quite a few arrests.

The cemetery had been in existence since the early 19th Century, and unlike the cemeteries of today with only headstones, it had quite a few large copper monuments and grave boundary markers. Several times while passing through the cemetery, I noticed some of the large monuments and grave markers disappearing, and requested to the sergeant if I could go in with an unmarked vehicle. Sergeant Smith granted my request and I was able to make several arrests. Later when I was assigned the burglary detail, my partner and I would stakeout the cemetery on occasion and made a few arrests; one of the incidents involved a police academy student.

Speaking about a police academy student, as I mentioned earlier, there were around thirty-five cops retiring or quitting per month. That put pressure on rehiring quickly, and the quality of the applicant wasn't always assured. Proof of that, one of my classmates was arrested while in the academy for driving a getaway car from a bank holdup. Another, after graduating and assigned to an affluent district, was arrested for being part of a burglary ring.

CHAPTER 4

Working a district

As time went on, members of 2 Squad would come and go almost without notice. Transfers usually occurred during your days off either by request, or departmental change, and most of the time the replacements were rookies. This was the hidden value of having veteran cops to learn from; certain things that only street experience will teach, and that aspect was slowly disappearing.

    I recall an incident when I probably had five years on the job. One 4 p.m. to midnight shift, a young cop by the name of Bill Yeager was assigned with me. Around 7 p.m., a radio call came out, "Man with a gun," and gave the address on Deal Street, a small street at the bottom of Lou's sector. It's a dead-end street of twelve foot front-row houses, with a sidewalk around 4' wide, and three steps to the front door.

    The street only accommodated one parking lane on the sidewalk along the abandoned factory opposite the homes, and to exit the street, you had to go to the end of the block where the people who lived there had a makeshift place to turn around. Like many streets in Frankford as well as older sections of Philadelphia, they were built strictly for horse and carriage use.

I was the first car on the scene, and noticed a guy with a handgun standing inside the front door of the house we were summoned to. Realizing we were going to be vulnerable, I stopped just short of the house, instructing Billy to take cover behind the vehicle and did likewise. With our guns drawn, I noticed Bill wasn't in a safe position, and made a poor choice of words by saying, "Shoot over there!" meaning to change to a safer position. With gun in hand he took my words literally as he turned to look around pointing his weapon in different directions, "Shoot where? Shoot where?" he replied.

Correcting myself, he did as I asked. Yelling to the male at the front door to drop the weapon, he only brandished it more by pointing it at us. Within a few minutes, Lou pulled up behind our vehicle. I yelled for Lou to take cover, but he came around his vehicle heading for the front door.

Realizing he must have known the residence and its occupants, we followed. After knocking at the front door, a different male opened it allowing us to enter. The gunman, after seeing Lou, pulled a fainting act falling to the floor in the living room. Lou responded with a kick in the ribs then picked up the blank gun being brandished and put it in his pocket.

Getting in the face of the other occupant he said, "The next time your brother pulls this shit, I'm going to lock you up." As we left the house I told Billy, "That's what having longevity on a sector means."

Although Billy and I hadn't remained in contact with one another due to him working the Mayfair section, whenever we met at reunions even years later, that incident always came up.

Older cops like Lou, the turnkey in the district Eddie Bunk, the gasman Jim Foody, and a few others in their mid to late fifties, younger cops referred to them as, "The over the hill gang."

They were patient as long as they weren't physically abused, and a group of bikers late one 4 p.m. to midnight shift one summer evening found out the hard way. They came to the district in mass to get several of their friends released from a charge of disorderly conduct, which took place at a local bar. The motorcyclist, were instructed to park their vehicles on the street instead of the driveway of the district.

While arguing with Jim Foody, a member of the group pushed him. Lou, Charlie Kamp, Frank Zornek, Eddie Bonk, and another older cop named Ricca, happened to be in the district handling assignments at the same time and went to his aid. They proceeded to beat the hell out of the bikers then physically removed the motorcycles without being gentle.

The adhesiveness between older and younger cops was evident, and I guess it had its roots imbedded when younger single cops would take less desirable details for older married cops. Christmas Eve and Christmas Day were one of these events. Generally, that holiday in particular was quiet, and everyone was allotted four hours off. Single cops like myself, would allow men with children to have the preference to which four hours they desired.

When one of the older cops by the name of Joe Kennedy was diagnosed with cancer, unsolicited, the entire squad en-mass went to the Philadelphia General Hospital where he was a patient to present him with an award.

With a quicker change of personnel in the squad, and the retirement of senior members, that seemed to end what I called the "Mayberry cohesiveness." Mayberry was a television show of a small town police department. That sort of togetherness kind of slowly dissolved as time passed. Little did I realize then, one of the reasons was we were becoming the older cops.

The squad on the lower end was a unique group who varied in years serving the department, and it seemed their character fit well with their assignment. Charlie Healy was the most senior as I mentioned earlier, and had been the beat cop from Bridge Street to Dyer Street for some twenty years or more. That included the bus and elevated train terminal, businesses, and three saloons. Like Lou, everyone knew Charlie.

I recall an incident on a Sunday day work, when I was walking a foot beat adjacent to his. At the time there, were what they called Sunday Blue Laws; no businesses were allowed to be open on Sunday. It was quiet that day just as most Sundays with little or no foot traffic. I happened to get to the intersection where our beats met and Charlie waved for me to join him. I noticed the door of the corner bar partially open and crossed the street to investigate with him. After pushing the door open, we stepped inside. There was a man behind the bar who appeared to be cleaning up and after looking at us he said, "Hey Charlie! What can I do for you?"

Realizing he was the owner, Charlie boldly said, "Since you're behind the bar you can pour me a whiskey. How about you, kid?" he asked.

"No thanks!" I replied.

"Suit yourself; it's part of my Irish heritage," Charlie replied with a chuckle.

Leaving the bar I laughed thinking, *If it was part of his Irish heritage he was in the right place.*

The name of the bar was Pat McGinnis's. The other bars on his beat were The Driftwood owned by Jack McConnell, and the Brown Jug Tavern owned by Charles Flannery.

I often wondered why older cops never wanted to take Sunday as a holiday, but it eventually dawned on me. Although prohibition was over ages ago, bars weren't open on Sunday and there was still a thriving enterprise in illegal liquor sales at speakeasies.

One case involved a call on Sunday to a hospital case in the 1700 block of Meadow Street. Upon arriving at the location, we noticed there was a man sitting on the curb with a bloody nose.

When I asked how it happened, he said another individual by the name of Charlie Barrett punched him while he was in Club Royal, putting an emphasis on the word *"Royalle."* There was no club operating in the district with that name to my knowledge, and after asking where it was, he directed us to a small row home on Plum Street. I knew by the size of the house there wouldn't be enough room to house such an operation, but he assured us there were about 20 people in the bar when it happened. After calling for the sergeant, I related the story.

After knocking at the door we were admitted by the home owner. We heard quite a ruckus in the rear-yard and hurried out the backdoor. To our surprise, we noticed a walkway leading to several connecting garages that fronted the next street. Opening the door, we noticed the partition walls between garages had been taken down, and a makeshift bar complete with stools, booths and a juke box were installed. The several people in the bar we let walk, but took the home owner and bartender to the district.

Just like the numbers racket, I thought those sort of crimes were a waste of time enforcing, but they were counted as vice arrests, and for some reason, higher ups in the department seemed to want to keep track of them. I truly believe it was a carryover from the days of prohibition, complete with graft for allowing it to happen, and wondered how many were still in operation throughout the city.

About every three months, we had to fill out what they called "vice reports." It became a joke for me, and for a complete year I made a report out on a numbers person who had been dead for at least that long.

There were several people who took numbers at different locations, and the person who stands out in my mind was a man nicknamed Tony the Barber. Tony was a short Italian immigrant who took numbers at the Frankford and Bridge Street Transportation Hub. He was evasive for one reason, Tony never wrote a daily number on paper; he kept probably several hundred in his head daily, and from what I was told, he never missed a payout. With that sort of talent, given a little education, he could have probably excelled in any endeavor.

He frustrated the police vice-squad command to a degree; they had a uniformed police officer assigned to follow him wherever he went. You were supposed to stay within ten feet of him so people couldn't give him a number and payment. As I said, I never believed numbers were a threat to our society and when assigned the detail, I told Tony to alert me when he was going to walk to a different area, so I could at least be somewhere in the vicinity in case the sergeant came by to check the detail. I knew other officers did the same so he complied with our request.

Tony worked the Northeast end of the Elevated Line, and a guy nicknamed the Pope, whose real name I've forgotten, worked the other end of the Elevated Line in West Philadelphia at the 69th Street Terminal. From what I understood, they were childhood friends with the head of the Philadelphia Mob, who at the time was Angelo Bruno. I also discovered Tony and the Pope were allowed to have their own enterprise not connected with the mob.

I happen to be speaking with Don Lee at the Bridge Street Terminal one Friday when Tony approached us and asked, "Do you guys play the horses?"

Surprised at his statement, we looked at each other then replied that we didn't. He continued by saying, "You guy's never really bothered me and I want to give you a tip. Take every dollar you have and put it on this horse, in the 5th race tomorrow at Delaware Park Racetrack."

After he walked away, we looked at each other, shrugged our shoulders, and continued our conversation about trout fishing. Saturday day-work came and went, and returning to day–work on Sunday, after roll-call Don asked, "Did you see the Sunday Paper?"

"No why?"

"That horse Tony told us about won that race. It paid $102 dollars."

This was 1972 and that sort of money to win was an anomaly. If there was ever a time I wanted to bang my head against a wall, it was after hearing that.

Several years later when I happened to get the detail again I asked,

"Tony, you gave me and Don Lee a horse to play at Delaware Park once. How did you know that horse was going to win?"

First looking down at the ground contemplating whether to answer my question, he looked up at me replying, "Kid, if I was younger I wouldn't tell you shit. I'm 80 years old and most of my friends are already dead. I'm tired of this city, and I'm going to Phoenix, Arizona, to live with my daughter."

For another moment he looked back down at his shoes, and I wondered whether he was thinking about guarding the secret he held. Finally looking back up at me he said, "That race was what we call in the rackets a 'boat-race.' It's for politicians and judges to get on."

With that, I watched as he slowly walked away, wondering whether he was thinking about the solemn oath he just violated many years ago to remain silent. Watching him walk cross the street I wondered what other interesting stories he had to tell.

Another interesting person, also an Italian immigrant, was a guy by the name of Gene Furtino. Gene owned a successful Pizza Shop at Frankford and Ruan Street, and also ran card games in the backroom of the shop where he lived.

I was on the beat where his store was one blustery cold February midnight to 8 a.m. shift. Just as he was about to close, I stepped into the shop to wait until he cleared the cash register. After he secured the money, he said in his heavy Italian accent as I was about to walk out the door. "It's cold outside. Here, don't freeze your ass off. Come inside once in awhile to get warm," handing me the key to the front door.

I looked at him briefly wondering whether I was the only one having that privilege, and realizing what I was thinking he said, "Don't worry; a few other young cops who walk the beat have one too."

Gene also took numbers at the store in competition with another guy by the nickname No-Coat-Joe. His real name was Joe Vergilliano and it seemed to be a running feud between the two of them for some reason that dated back years.

A funny story about Gene happened several years after I was assigned 1501 police wagon with Jesse. Just after roll-call one 4 p.m. to midnight shift; the cop that worked the sector car where the pizza shop is located approached Jess and I waiting in line to refuel.

He said, "Hey you guys, I heard the inspector's men talking about raiding Gene's Pizza Shop for a card game going on. Get down there and warn him."

"John, I'm almost out of gas. You'll have to do it," I replied.

Following him into the district, we stepped into a small room that wasn't being used to make the call. After dialing the number, I heard John say, "Gene, this is John Demarko, stop the card game the inspector's men are coming to raid the joint." After a few seconds, he frustratingly repeated his statement.

After he hung up the phone I asked, "Is he stopping the game?"

Looking at me he replied, "I don't know, all he kept saying in his heavy Italian accent was, 'This a Gena. This is Gena. Whattya you want?' He thinks I'm trying to order a pizza."

After being refueled, we received a radio call to meet the inspector's men with prisoners at the Pizza Shop. Hearing the call, we realized the raid must have been successful and headed to the store. Upon arrival, as we guessed, the inspector's men were there with several people handcuffed. After placing the prisoners in the police wagon, our uniform sergeant who was also at the scene, waved for me to bring him our duty log to sign, a function for the sergeant on every tour of duty.

While standing next to the sergeant's car, John pulled up in his patrol-car. The sergeant seeing him, waived for him to bring his log too, and John brought it across the street to where we were standing. The sergeant handed me my log back and took John's. While he was signing John's log he candidly looked up at him and asked, "John, whose side are you on?"

"What do you mean Sarge?" John replied.

Looking at John to see what his reaction would be the sergeant said in a forced Italian accent, "This a Gena. This a Gena. A whattya you want?"

Embarrassed, not knowing what to say, John just stood there with an open mouth. Without saying it, I realized the sergeant as well as most of the younger cops didn't think vice was a big deal. I knew I wouldn't be able to stifle my laughter, so I quickly walked back to the police wagon.

CHAPTER 5

Two Squad

Getting back to describing the squad, a few other members were Walt Singer, who worked the Bridesburg section in 153 Car. Walt was a tall, lanky sort of fellow in his late thirties. His sector bordered the Delaware River on the east and Tacony Street on the west, probably the least active car in the lower end. It was one of those closely-knit Polish neighborhoods where you would see row house owners on Saturday, scrubbing their white marble front-steps. The sector was also comprised of heavy industry, chemical companies, and a dozen trucking firms, and also one of the largest junkyards in the city. Walt would later be shot to death with his own revolver by a family member over a domestic dispute.

The neighboring sector to 153 was 154. It was manned by a policeman named Tony Lewin. The nickname given to him was Tony Hot Comb, and I assumed it was because he was nice looking and always conscious of his hair. Tony's sector was also heavy with industry, and the few residential sections were mainly people of Italian and Ukrainian descent. His sector was from Tacony Street on the east side, to Torressdale Avenue on the West, and from Bridge Street on the north end, to Adams Avenue on the south end. He had a street at the bottom of his sector inhabited by a pretty rough group. If one had the ability to relocate it, it would fit right into a neighborhood like Dog Patch, strictly hillbilly. The "dirty-neckers," as we referred to them, were a rough group of people perpetually involved in one way or another with stolen autos and auto parts. Tony spent much of his time monitoring the street.

At the time, there was a police comedy television show called, "Car 54, where are you?" and Tony took quite a bit of harassment about that.

I recall an assignment of a burglary in progress on his sector at a bicycle shop on Tacony Street around 3 a.m. I went in on the assignment and covered the front while he ran up the side alley of the store to cover the back. Within a few minutes, he returned holding a guy by the scruff of the neck. The guy seemed to be dazed touching what was rapidly becoming a lump on his head. Getting his senses he said, "I'm the owner of the shop. I'm the one who called the police."

Apparently, he was coming out the back door of the shop when Tony wacked him with his nightstick before the guy could identify himself. Luckily we retrieved a few bicycles in the next alley, and after returning them, the guy didn't press the issue, and we left without further complaint.

The next person in the squad I'd like to describe is Dave Tulley. Dave was also a tall thin lanky person originally from Arizona, who spoke with a western-drawl. He was one of those personalities that without trying, his dry humor made you laugh.

He was in the Navy stationed on a ship being repaired at the Philadelphia Navy Yard, and while there, met his future wife. After being discharged from the military, they married and he joined the police department. For some reason after a year on the job, he decided to go back to Arizona and joined the Phoenix Police Department, but within six months he returned probably by a suggestion from his wife. The remarkable part of his adventure, he not only returned to the same district, but the same squad and the same car assignment, something unusual in those days.

Although Dave had a slow western-drawl, make no mistake, he was wiry when it came to being physical. I once rolled in on a disturbance call he received where he was pummeling the hell out of a guy almost twice his size in the middle of the street. The guy made the mistake of trying to take on Dave, one on one.

His sector covered the lower end from where Torresdale Avenue and Frankford Avenue meet, to Orthodox Street, sort of a pie-slice shaped sector. His area comprised several industrial firms, and the inhabitants were people with a mixture of different backgrounds, Italian, Irish and some ethnic groups, primarily welfare and lower scale working class people.

I recall an incident where we were working the midnight to 8 a.m. shift. It was winter and during the last part of the tour it rained briefly; then quickly froze, causing a thin coating of ice on everything including the streets and sidewalks. My partner at the time was Jesse, and we were working 1501 police wagon. Around 7 a.m., Dave got a call to a disturbance house in the 1300 block of Sellers Street where we backed him up. Sellers Street is a one-way narrow street with parking on both sides, and the 1300 block in particular, has a steep downhill grade emptying out onto a two way street, and across the intersection is a railroad siding.

Dave reached the assignment ahead of us and without a parking space he stopped in the middle of the street at the top of the hill. I pulled in behind him and after handling the assignment, we returned to our vehicles slipping and sliding on the ice covered ground. Dave said, "I'm not moving my vehicle until the city spreads some salt on this street."

Being behind his vehicle I couldn't back out or go forward. Jesse, wanting to report off boasted, "Dave, give me the keys. I'll show you how we used to do it in Alaska."

We both knew he was never in the military, but Dave smiled handing him the keys, and Jesse got in the car and started the engine. Standing behind the vehicle, Dave and I noticed the backup lights go on then break lights as he put it in gear. The car didn't go ten feet when the brake lights came on immediately. Watching the rear lights, we knew he was pumping the brakes to no avail, and the car continued to pick up speed going downhill. It first swerved to the left striking a parked vehicle. Coming back to the right, it sideswiped another and continued downhill careening off a few more, before reaching the end of the block. Luckily, the car went through the intersection without having an accident from cross traffic, and wound up in the railroad siding.

Getting out of the car unscathed, Jesse first looked at the damage to the police car then up the hill at us. Seeing he was uninjured, Dave put his hands on his hips. He laughingly said out loud with his slow western drawl, "Hey Jess! Is that how they used to do it in Alaska?"

The next sector north of 155 was 158. The boundaries were from Orthodox Street in the South, to Harrison Street on the North, from Torresdale Avenue on the East, to Frankford Avenue on the West, the busiest sector in the district. It encompassed a public housing project, a junior high school and several other trouble spots.

It was a neighborhood in transition with quite a few older people who were long time residents in Frankford. The makeup of younger people moving into the area was pretty much equal, black and white with a few Hispanic and a few Orientals. These were mainly lower-wage poorer class people with quite a few reliant on public welfare.

The cops assigned that sector were Donald Lee, an Oriental, and Jesse Strange, who was black, who would eventually become my partner. Lee was around six foot tall, and on the heavy side. Sitting in the police car with his hands folded on his lap, he looked like Buddha, a nickname the black people in the project coined. Jesse was around five ten and stocky built. They both had a calm demeanor with a sense of humor, which was a necessity for working their sector.

I recall an incident where I replaced Jesse on a 4 p.m. to midnight shift for some reason. Don and I received a call to a disturbance in the housing project, where apparently he was used to getting calls, something police get familiar with over time.

After being admitted, the middle age complainant began her usual triad about an alcoholic husband. Don, noticing a guitar leaning against the wall, picked it up and began to play. The complainant frustratingly sat down on a kitchen chair saying, "I'll be damn. I dun called the police and he comes in here, picks up the damn guitar and starts pickin.'"

After finishing her remarks Don said, "Elvira, if that's all, I'll see you next 4 to 12," then we left.

Don was normally a calm guy by nature but make no mistake; when riled he had no problem demonstrating his strength. We had an assignment that same night of a fight and disturbance in a bar. The person we had to take into custody seemed to be high on a combination of alcohol and drugs of some sort. He looked to be in his mid twenties, six feet tall and at least 200 pounds. He had a head wound from the confrontation he was in and was getting out of hand. It was an extremely busy night, and there were no police wagons immediately available, so we took him in our vehicle to the emergency room for treatment. As we were placing him in the rear seat of the police car, he began to get violent, so we put handcuffs on him for our own safety. After arriving at the hospital, we escorted him to a treatment area with curtain dividers separating two beds. The attending physician, after speaking gently with the patient, asked us to remove the handcuffs and wait in the hall. We warned the doctor about the patient having emotional swings and could become violent, but the doctor insisted he would be fine, and asked us again to leave the treatment area. As soon as we removed the handcuffs, the patient grabbed the doctor by the throat and began to strangle him. The patient fell to the floor while getting off the gurney and Don grabbed him by the arm and one leg. Physically picking him up over his head just as if he was lifting a barbell in a weight lifting competition, he bounced the prisoner back on the gurney and said to him, "If you do it again, you're really going to need treatment."

The prisoner calmly sat while he was being treated and after the doctor was finished, we drove the prisoner to the district. Later, I discovered the attending physician was studying to be a psychiatrist, which was probably why he thought he could handle the patient with kind words.

The next and final car of the lower end was 159. Its area of assignment was Harrison Street on the south, Cheltenham Avenue on the north, and from Torresdale in the east, to Frankford Avenue on the west. The car was manned by a veteran officer named Dick Weston, a man in his mid forties with graying hair. His sector was comprised mainly of middle class wage earners. When a new group of officers came to the squad, he was replaced by one of the rookies, and became the detail cop at Harding Junior High School.

Last but not least, the police wagons which patrolled the lower end. They were 1502, with Hank Jones and Danny Powell, both with seniority in the department. They covered the territory of 153 and 154.

Police Wagon 1501 was manned by Jimmy Balmer and Bob Rice both pretty tough veteran officers in their late thirties. They covered the sectors of 155, 158 and 159, the highest number car in the lower end. Jimmy would eventually go up in rank and return as the lieutenant of two squad. Frank Zornek and Charlie Kamp worked 1500 wagon and covered the sectors of 156 and 157.

Other foot beat officers were Charlie Healey, Scotty Couglin, a Scottish immigrant in his early 50's, and William Robertson, a well presented tall black officer in his mid-twenties. Robbie, as we referred to him, was a former paratrooper honorably discharged from the Army.

I wasn't in the district very long and hadn't received my permanent assignment, when I was assigned a police car with Scotty Couglin. It was the midnight to 8 a.m. shift, and he was parked on Wakeling Street watching a bar called the Brown Jug on Frankford Avenue. I first thought he may have been watching the establishment for serving minors, but after an hour, we watched as a patron left the bar. He appeared to be having difficulty opening his car door, dropping the keys several times, and after getting in, he started the engine and began driving down the street. Scotty immediately followed and within a few blocks he signaled the car to pull over.

As any car stop, I exited and took a position on the passenger side as Scotty spoke to the driver. Speaking to each other, they sounded like an echo; the driver also had a Scottish accent. After a little more conversation, it was discovered they were both from the same area in Scotland. Ending the conversation, Scotty said in his Brogue, "It's nice to know where you're from now Laddie, but it sure doesn't buy me breakfast now, does it?"

Shaking my head, I returned to the vehicle. I thought for a moment I better served John Q Public when I was in Task Force.

The lieutenant of the squad was Jim Monfort, a unique character in the respect; he came up in a neighborhood in the city called the "brickyard." How it got its name is a mystery to me to this day, but if it had anything to do with his toughness, that may have been its origin. He was a man in his early forties around six feet tall and in tremendous shape. From what I was told, he was a former prize-fighter. He would clear his throat with,

"Ahhhm," before speaking, and I wasn't sure whether it was to get your full attention or just out of habit.

He drove a salmon-colored Hearse as his everyday automobile, something everyone but him thought was unusual.

The clerical end of the squad were office personnel we referred to as "the inside crew." They manned the district and took care of the paperwork for the squad. The ranking person was a Corporal whose last name was Roach. He had several assistants named Phil Lowe, and John Derbyshire. Eddie Bonk was the turnkey for the cell-room, and Jim Footy was the gas-man. That in a nutshell was the inside crew and the lower end personnel.

CHAPTER 6

The J/R

I had several assignments where Lieutenant Monfort was present, and one sticks out above all others. There were four active nightclubs in the lower-end and two were on my sector. One was the Jade East at Griscom and Oxford Avenue, and the other was the Juniata/Republican Club in the 4700 block of Frankford Avenue. The word Republican had nothing to do with politics, but the club was unique in its own way. The J/R as we called it, used to be a popular hangout for off duty cops on one side of the bar, and people who were mainly roofers with arrest records for burglary and so forth, on the other. Every midnight to 8 a.m. shift, I had to take myself out of service and enter the club at 2:50 a.m. This was to insure it observed the rule of the Liquor Control Board and stop serving drinks at 3 o'clock.

As 3 a.m. approached, the patrons would order two and three drinks and sit until they were consumed. Stationing myself by the front door next to the cloakroom, I was able to get a broad view of the bar area. At around 3:15 when the last patrons were still hanging out, I would open the electrical panel box and begin throwing the main circuit breaker off and on in rapid succession yelling, "Come on people... time to go!" This usually finished the tolerance of the last few, and to the bartender's delight, the place would begin to empty.

One of the toughest things to deal with closing the club was people who were intoxicated wanting to express their gratitude for me being a cop. For one reason or another, they insisted doing it with their hands on my shoulders speaking several inches from my face. On one occasion, there was a girl who was obviously intoxicated adamant to want to kiss me. After telling her not to, she closed her eyes and leaned forward with the attempt. I slipped from beneath her outstretched arms as she leaned forward and wound up kissing the Jukebox then fell to the floor. There were other instances that were humorous, too many to mention, but there were also more serious instances.

While closing the club, I had several occasions where information was past to me by someone leaving about another patron they disliked. One night, I had a formally convicted burglar I knew by the nickname of Apples tell me as he quietly passed, "I heard the two at the end of the bar, Joe Stocker and Marty Bell talking about knocking off the American Legion Post on Leiper Street tonight." Looking towards that end of the bar, I knew both Stocker and Bell to have past records for burglary and believed Apples to be telling the truth.

After the bar emptied, I called for the lieutenant and told him what was said. He had several cars and a police wagon go out of service and told us his plan to surround the building. After several of us got in the police wagon, we proceeded to the Legion Post. After arriving, we quickly exited and positioned ourselves around the building.

The Legion Post that was converted to a club was formerly a mansion of an affluent family that once lived in Frankford. It sat on a large lot with a lot of lawn, trees, and bushes around the building. Tony Lewin and I were on the darker side, and other officers covered the remaining sides.

The lieutenant and wagon crew found the rear door of the property open and apprehended Stocker almost immediately.

After putting him in the wagon, the lieutenant came around to our side of the building. I asked if they apprehended both; and as he said, "No!" Suddenly drawing his revolver, Tony and I looked at each other not knowing what to expect. The lieutenant, looking up at the ledge of the second floor of the building, pointed his weapon and flashlight and said "Now jump!"

Turning around to look up, Marty Bell was standing quietly on a ledge just above Tony and I the whole time we were there, never making a sound. He didn't comply with the lieutenant at first, but after the lieutenant cocked the hammer of his revolver, Marty complied. He hit the ground rolling, and never injured himself. That was one of several instances I had at the J/R Club.

Marty Bell was one of the more colorful characters who patronized the J/R. Several years before, when I was new walking the beat on Frankford Avenue, I discovered an open rear door of a Singer Sewing Machine Store located at the time in the 4500 block. After stepping inside, I saw a shadow quickly moving to my right. I drew my revolver and scanned the room. Realizing whoever it was, was within hearing distance of me cocking the hammer, I yelled out, "If I have to find you, you're a dead man."

Realizing I was new in the district, Marty didn't want to take a chance, and quickly stepped from the shadows.

Another person passing me information was John Boggs, a man with a long criminal record. One night as he was leaving the club he said, "The guy at the end of the bar Phil Corr, said he was going to kill George Morris after they leave the Club."

I don't recall the reason, but it wouldn't have been unlikely they were in some kind of caper together, and one felt cheated for some reason or another. After Phil left, I followed him out the door and shoved him against the police car. Frisking him, I retrieved a .32 Caliber Pistol from his coat pocket. After taking him to Detective Headquarters, they ran the serial number of the weapon through N.C.I.C., a central bank where information is stored about crimes involving personal property. It was discovered the gun was reported stolen from a burglary of a business several weeks before.

The majority of the patrons in the J/R were mainly from the Kensington section of the city, or what we call the K & A neighborhood, the initials standing for the intersection of Kensington and Allegheny Avenue. The make-up of the people were working class Irish, Polish with a few other nationalities mixed in. Make no mistake about the suspected low level of intellect of these individuals; they had the FBI baffled for several years. It seemed their normal lifestyle and supposed low level of intelligence, was a perfect disguise for burglaries being committed from New England, to Florida along the east coast, and as far west as Ohio. They were burglarizing homes of wealthy people, and the FBI in Washington was completely at a loss for solving the crimes.

The only way they were caught, was taking a person who was never a part of the original group on what they call a caper. They always traveled independently to a location where they staked out several homes for burglary, and after targeting the homes they wanted, they would check into a motel nearby. Apparently, they had a system of what to take and what to leave behind. The morning they were to return to K & A after burglarizing several homes, the leader of the group noticed the new person had taken a few Mink Stoles from one of the houses. He was told to get rid of them before leaving the motel, and the new person made the mistake of throwing them in the motel dumpster. Someone observing it called the police and the rest was history. I think the total in jewelry and cash taken over several years was several million dollars. Subsequently they were all arrested.

CHAPTER 7

Jesse

In late 1969, Don Lee was assigned a foot beat by choice, and I was his replacement on 158. That began a seven-year assignment as a partner with Jesse. *"The Jess,"* as I referred to him, and I, became a great team just as Iron Mike and me.

Jesse used to say, "I used to hate coming to work on the 4 to 12, but you always give me a reason to laugh."

He was referring to the fact most of the time I took police work lightly, always finding a little humor in things. I have the ability to imitate people's voices and also have the ability to act in many ways like the person or persons we dealt with. More than once when I was interviewing someone on a less serious assignment and went into one of my acts, Jesse would have to walk away to keep from laughing out loud.

One small example is a call we received to a residence for a domestic disturbance and a hospital case. It was summer and the front door of the residence was open so we stepped inside. There was a young male sitting on the sofa with his legs crossed wearing a pink jump suit, nonchalantly filing his nails. Jesse asked, "Did you call the police for a hospital case?"

The male replied, "Yes! The bitch is in the kitchen," pointing in that direction.

I replied in the same tone, "Well, I guess we'll just have to go and see."

Walking into the kitchen we observed a middle-aged white male who appeared to be waking from a blow to the head. We suspected the knot beginning to appear, was from a frying-pan lying on the floor next to him. After getting his bearings Jesse asked, "What happened?"

With an English accent straight from the streets of London he replied, "She! Or rather he; struck me!"

I answered in the same English accent, "My! My! Governor, it seems as though you got yourself into a bit of a sticky wicket."

Jesse couldn't get outside fast enough trying to stifle his laughter and seeing his reaction, caused me to lose some of my composure. I was happy the Englishman was still half-dazed to notice.

There were other times when humor had to be stifled and another in particular, was a 4 p.m. to midnight shift when I was still on 157. It was an extremely warm summer evening that was pretty busy. Pulling behind a fast-food restaurant to get a meal to go, I observed an auto with all the windows down with two males sitting in it. It was at the far end of the parking lot and I thought to investigate after retrieving my dinner.

Before I could exit the car, a call of a holdup in progress went out, and I sped away to the scene. The holdup wasn't in progress; it had already taken place. After cruising the area for awhile looking for suspects, without success, I went back to the restaurant.

The car I observed earlier was still there with the windows rolled down, but it appeared the males were gone. Suspecting the car may have been stolen; I took my flashlight and walked to where the car was parked. I heard noises from inside the vehicle and shined my flashlight in on two males face down in the rear seat involved in what appeared to be sodomy by buggery.

After tapping my flashlight on the door they both jumped up. Checking whether the car was stolen, I read the tag to the dispatcher. In a few minutes, Jesse hearing the call pulled up next to me.

One of the males had a bench warrant for failing to appear in court and I called for a police wagon to transport the occupants to the district. The one that was the doer had the warrant, and seeing his arrest record I wasn't about to let it pass. He had several arrests for burglary, a few drug arrests, and one for assault and battery on a cop. I filled out the paperwork and the detective doing the arrest report mentioned I'd have to testify if the case went to court. "I have no problem with that," I replied.

The day of the court-notice Jesse happened to be in another courtroom on a separate case, but came into the room I was in and took a seat in the front row. I knew he was only there for one purpose. Knowing my demeanor, he wanted to see how I would testify.

The judge, seeing the charges, must have had a prior discussion with the Assistant District Attorney to have the case called first.

After the court officer announced the court was in session, the conversations in the room faded. Very seriously addressing the defendants the judge said, "Do you realize the maximum punishment for these offenses could be a fine of ten thousand dollars or ten years imprisonment?"

The courtroom was packed with people for lesser offenses, and as soon as the judge said it, the room fell silent, everyone wondering what the case was about. The Assistant District Attorney called me to the stand to relate the case, and as soon as I began my testimony, I saw Jesse lean forward trying to stifle his laughter. After presenting my testimony the defendant's lawyer began to question me, something I didn't expect. One of the questions was, "Officer did you actually observe penetration?"

Obviously not being able to I replied, "No councilor, but there were moans and groans of what sounded like pleasure of the defendant on the bottom."

The courtroom erupted in laughter and the judge immediately spun around in his chair heading for his chambers. I broke slightly with a grin after seeing the courtroom's reaction, but Jesse wasn't able to control his laughter and quickly exited the room.

When the judge finally regained his composure and returned, he ordered the defendant with the bench warrant detained, and released the other male. Leaving the courtroom, Jesse was in the hall still laughing and said, "Sorry Randy, I couldn't help but laugh. That answer even broke the judge's demeanor."

My testimony was good and I was never reluctant to describe an interaction whether it be good or bad. Lawyers will try to paint a situation where the cop appears to be wrong, and most cops fall for that tactic not wanting to sound overzealous.

One example was Jesse and I backing up another cop on a disturbance call on the third floor apartment over a bar in the 1600 block of Orthodox Street. The cop we were backing was in his mid fifties almost ready to retire. Policeman Ricca was already in the apartment when we crested the stairs to the third floor.

The apartment door was open and we saw a woman standing in the living room holding a bloody towel over what appeared to be a split-lip. We had been at the apartment before on disturbances so we were familiar with the situation. The person she was living with was a white male in his late twenties, over six feet tall and weighed about 240 pounds. He was a roofers-union goon known for a bad temper, and had several arrests for assault and battery on police, plus several burglary arrests.

He was about to go after the woman again when Ricca touched his forearm asking him to calm down. He looked at Ricca's hand and stated, "That's my arm," then punched Ricca, sending him across the room where he hit the wall and fell behind the sofa.

Looking at Jesse and I he said, "Nigger, you're next!" and came at us, grabbing Jesse. I side-stepped, hitting him on the head with my nightstick as hard as I could. It was enough to loosen his grip on Jesse and went to his knees.

Shaking it off he said, "When I get to my feet I'll kick both your asses."

Ricca was coming up from behind the couch after being knocked out, and it temporarily distracted him from going after Jesse again, so I gave him another shot to the head.

Going to his knees a second time he said again, "When I get to my feet, I'll kick all your asses." Giving him several more hits, it finally dazed him enough to put the handcuffs on. Taking him downstairs in no gentle manner, we called for a police wagon to take him to the emergency room for treatment. Ricca also had to be driven to the hospital for treatment.

When we got to the district, the prisoner was booked, and like everyone who's arrested, he had to go to an arraignment at the Police Administration Building. At central-cell they photograph and fingerprint the offender for obvious reasons. When the case went to court, I was the testifying officer since I was the one most instrumental with the arrest. After testifying to what happened the defense attorney asked, "Officer, how many times did you strike my client, was it once, twice?" Something the photos taken before the arraignment would clearly dispute.

I had been in court many times and heard cops not wanting to appear overzealous sound ridiculous. It only adds to the reason for not believing their testimony which didn't make sense to me. My answer was always truthful and I would reply if asked that question, "It was probably more than three, possibly four or five. I don't really remember, as many times as it took to take control of the situation."

Generally that would end the questions.

Even in sequestration, Jesse and I were good at testifying, and more than once, defending lawyers would be stumped with our answers.

For example, if I was asked, "Officer, how fast were you patrolling; when you observed my client?" I would reply, "Very slow, maybe three or four miles an hour." When Jesse was asked the same question he would reply, "Walk speed," basically the same; but different descriptions.

There were other tricks to our testimony that usually sealed the fate of the defendant, and as more than one lawyer said as we were leaving the courtroom, "You guys are good."

Judges are the best critic when it comes to testimony; they hear so much of it. We were in court so often; a few judges familiar with us realized we came prepared. We were sometimes told by other officers present in the same courtroom we were good with our testimony, and that was always gratifying to hear.

I recall a case where a defense attorney couldn't get around my testimony and said with a shrug of his shoulders to the judge, "Your Honor. What can I do? What more can I say?"

The judge replied, "Nothing. I guess your client's guilty."

That brought a laugh even from the Assistant District Attorney.

In another instance, a new district attorney describing a case kept saying, "He said this, and he said that," instead of saying the person's name. The judge finally getting tired of hearing, "He said," asked,

"You keep saying he said. Who's he?"

The D. A. replied, "Him!" pointing at the defendant.

The judge replied, "Well, say him!"

The very next statement the lawyer replied, "Him, said." Everyone in the courtroom laughed, and the judge just shook his head.

Every cop on the street has a pet peeve, and mine was violence against older people who fell victim to it during a purse snatch or beat up and robbed. As I mentioned, there were quite a few older residents living in the area who couldn't afford to escape the change in the neighborhood, and these were the most vulnerable and an easy target for robbery or purse-snatches.

The city set up a methadone clinic in the 4600 block of Paul Street just off the avenue to dispense medicine to so called reforming junkies, but the truth in the matter, most of them only wanted to be part of the program to cut back their habit. Every morning a crowd from different parts of the city would gather waiting for it to open, and it was probably the main reason purse snatches and robberies of older people became a regular event. At the time, I carried a straight razor for cutting the nylon string used to hang or remove temporary no parking signs. If a perpetrator had a ponytail and roughed up an older victim, I would take a lock of their hair.

I recall an arrest where an older woman was thrown to the ground after getting her purse snatched, suffering a fractured wrist and hip. We caught the guy who was armed with a knife and he had a long ponytail, so I took a lock. Several days later, there was another robbery where the victim was beat-up severely. When we caught that perpetrator he too had long hair, so I took a lock.

Several weeks later, I was summoned to Common Pleas Court for the first purse snatch. I had several cases before the same judge in the past and he was familiar with me. After the defendant was found guilty the judge asked, "Is there anything you'd like to say before sentencing?"

The defendant replied, "Yes, your honor. That officer cut my hair."

The judge looked at him with skepticism and after looking at his record, sentenced him to 18 to 23 three months in the house of correction.

The following week, I had the second case of the robbery and beating of the complainant before the same judge. After finding the defendant guilty, he asked if there was anything the defendant had to say. He too, mentioned getting his ponytail lopped off. After sentencing the judge leaned over to me quietly saying, "Do you want to be a cop or a fucking barber? Get rid of the straight razor.

There was another notable funny incident which took place in court. I was working solo on a 4 p.m. to midnight shift, and made an arrest of a strong-arm robbery. I was about to go on vacation and didn't want it interrupted, so I signed Jesse's name as the arresting officer. When I returned from vacation, Jesse filled me in on what transpired in the courtroom over that case. He said when he received the court notice, he couldn't remember the case. In court, he said the defendant with his long record pleaded guilty trying to evade a long sentence. Jesse never told me the sentence, but mentioned the defendant saying to the judge afterward, "Your Honor, that's not the officer who arrested me. It was a white cop."

After the case was over, the assistant district attorney asked Jesse why the defendant made that statement. Jesse told me, "I had to quickly think of an answer so I said, 'I guess the guy was so drugged up, maybe he was confused.'

With the size of the court system in Philadelphia there was an anomaly. It seemed like we had quite a few cases before the same judge, and several times he would lean toward us after taking the stand and ask, "Officer, what kind of case is this?"

After giving him the highlights of the case there wasn't much room for rebuttal. Jesse and I never took anyone down unless we were pretty much guaranteed a conviction. If there was a gray area of possibly an acquittal, we settled for information on anything illegal in the neighborhood, mainly the sale of heroin.

A good example of not being able to make an arrest without an informant was about a woman who went around the neighborhood pushing her young daughter in a baby carriage. Barbara was dealing heroin from the coach and had been doing it for several years. After her arrest, we discovered she was strung-out using four bags of heroin daily. At that time, a bag, which is one dose, cost $8 and she was doing what we call "dumping," four bags daily. That amounts to a $32 per day, and seven-day-a week habit. Drug habits don't take weekends off, and the path to supporting your habit if you're a female would be dealing drugs, shoplifting, prostitution or all three. Most males resorted to dealing dope, burglary and robbery, shoplifting on occasion.

CHAPTER 8

Warrants

The lower end was getting extremely busy while Jesse and I were assigned 158 car, and the sergeant asked who I thought would be a good replacement on 157. I recommended another cop currently assigned the Mayfair area, a former Marine by the name of John Galliano, who turned out to be the right choice. Between him, Jesse and I, we were able to keep pressure on drug activity and crime in the lower end.

We taught Galliano what we knew about warrants and familiarized him with the people in the Frankford section. While working as a team, we made many felony arrests. Part of that reason, Jesse and I were from the same neighborhood in North Philly. Although we didn't know each other there, there were people we knew from our old neighborhood moving into the White Hall Housing project, and surrounding area. Victorian homes converted into rooming houses were also havens for transient people.

Search warrants for one of the more memorable arrests, was for a house where heroin was being sold on Tackawanna Street. The plural for warrants, we hit the same house several times in the month of February, and came up with large quantities of heroin and on several occasions, guns. It was an old Victorian-type single home that had multiple uses.

They were not only using it as a house for distributing heroin, it was also being used for prostituting younger girls, often drug users, mainly underage runaways. Some of them were also used as runners to take packets of heroin to different locations for street dealers. In referring to prostitution, it wasn't organized prostitution in that sense of the word, but strictly to support their heroin habit.

Quite a few times before going on the street 4 p.m. to midnight, the corporal would ask Jesse and I to speak with a concerned parent or guardian who came to the district inquiring about a sibling who ran away for one reason or another.

After showing us a picture of a child some as young as thirteen, they would ask if we happened to see them. Their anticipation of a positive response was always cause for not telling the complete truth. We would take the picture and if we saw them and they were underage, we would take them into the district. Inevitably, we would discover track marks on their arms and with a little pressure, would discover other runaways being harbored in the same house being used for prostitution.

Most of our warrants were made out and served on the 4 p.m. to midnight, or midnight to 8 a.m. shift. The warrants were pretty much ironclad and the chances of being disputed in court were almost nonexistent. The person instrumental with teaching us how to make out warrants was a former high school classmate who became a criminal lawyer. Not long after teaching us, he turned informant giving evidence to the F.B.I. about drug dealing in the city, and as a result, for his own safety, was sent out west to live under the federal witness protection program.

In those days I had a small concrete business as a side job, and one of my tools was a twenty-five-pound sledgehammer. It was also the perfect tool for breaking down doors when executing warrants. Being pretty strong, I would swing the hammer with all my might striking the hinge side of the door. One swing was usually violent enough to send the door five feet into the living room. On one occasion upon a quick entry serving a warrant, everyone in the living room immediately took a seat on the sofa. After commanding them to move, we found almost five hundred small packets of heroin and two hand guns. There were also two teenage runaways on the second floor, one sexually active.

Narcotics arrests weren't very difficult as the area was becoming rife with that kind of activity. I recall in 1971 or 1972, Jesse and I, through an informant, heard of several people we were familiar with bringing a kilo of heroin into Frankford. Through the informant, we heard it was purchased in New York, and he told us the exact location where it was going to be broken down and bagged for street sale, an apartment on the second floor in the 1600 block of Orthodox Street. Working the day shift, we set in motion the process of getting a warrant. I don't recall the reason, but it was difficult to get together in a hurry and we didn't get it completed until late in the shift.

The day-work shift had just ended and Jesse, Galliano, and I, were in the locker room discussing how we were going to go about executing the warrant. Lou, who was hanging his gear in his locker approached us and asked, "Hey kids! Are you going to serve that warrant?"

"Yeah Lou! Why?" I replied.

"You're off duty. Unless the city wants to keep you on the payroll, I wouldn't bother. If you get shot or injured, the city's not going to back you. They'll say you did it on your own time."

Jesse and I looked at each other, and realizing he was probably right, decided to forget the idea. As a result, there were several fatal overdoses within the next several weeks.

As time passed, we were gathering more informants and pretty much knew everything that was going on in the lower end. Who was selling, who was supplying, and so forth. Suppliers would keep changing locations trying to stay ahead of what we were learning, but with the informants we had, we were able to stay pretty close to the changes.

Another memorable arrest was on the 4600 block of Penn Street. The house was an older twin with a glass enclosed front porch. For several nights of the 4 p.m. to midnight shift, I would station myself in a darkened section down the block to watch the various people entering and exiting within a short period of time. It was February, and the temperature was in the low 20's, and periodically Jesse would take my place. Observing the drug people we knew going in and out of the house for several days was enough probable cause to obtain a search warrant.

The sidewalk going to the front door was common through the small front yard and split in two directions serving each home. The yard had a high hedge fence which obscured the bottom half of the enclosed porch and proved to be great cover.

On the way to serve the warrant, a male by the name of Charles Hoffman was coming from the front yard and we quickly took him into custody, not wanting him to call the supplier, giving away our intent. Looking for a place to secure him, without success, I handcuffed him to an iron railing secured in a set of concrete steps around the corner. We then proceeded to serve the warrant. After getting the phone number from Hoffman's wallet, I used the public telephone close by. With altering my voice to sound like him, I was able to convince the party inside the house I was coming back, over a miscount of heroin I received.

Taking his cap and jacket we went back to the house. After ringing the bell, I stood with my back to the front door. To my surprise, the occupant opened the door before looking to see who I was. After rushing him and knocking him down, we quickly entered. There were several people in the house and we gathered them together in the living room. While searching the house for heroin, the phone rang and I disguised my voice to sound like the dealer. The conversation was about who they were and how much heroin they wanted. After hanging up the phone I went out to the front yard and positioned myself behind the hedge fence once again.

The enclosed porch had large glass windows with shades and one shade covered the almost full length glass front door. When the caller got to the front door and rang the bell, to their surprise, Jesse would open the door. As they turned to run I would hit them with a full block in the back, sending them headlong into the enclosed porch. Before we were finished that evening, we had seven street dealers, the supplier, and a lot of heroin.

After calling for a police wagon to transport them Jesse said, "Hey Randy, we left Hoffman handcuffed to the steps around the corner."

Serving the warrant, we had forgotten all about him and when we released him, he was about half frozen.

During the first several years working the lower end of the district, there was a noticeable amount of people leaving the neighborhoods, being replaced with less desirable people. That would eventually be the case with most of the eastside and part of the west-side of the lower end during my time there.

As time went on, it became increasingly easier to make drug arrests due to the heavy traffic of white kids coming to the project from the northeast and suburbs to purchase it. The White Hall Public Housing Project is a multi-unit complex on both sides of Tackawanna Street, from Margaret Street to Harrison Street, with many avenues of entrances and exits, extremely difficult to cover. Once in awhile we would have an informant tell us a direct target and would get lucky but not often.

Quite a few informants would give us information for not being arrested for something we had a strong suspicion they did, and one example was working the midnight to 8 a.m. shift in 158 Car. For some reason, Jesse was off that night and I was solo. Around 4 a.m., I pulled up on a known junkie walking down the street by the name of Tommy.

Tommy had given us information in the past to avoid arrest which was part of Jesse and my policy. If we didn't have someone 100% we settled for whatever information they would offer. While talking with him, I noticed a white substance on his fingers that looked like paint. It wasn't unheard of for a junkie to help one of the local contractors painting, or some other means of gaining a few dollars to support a habit. After our conversation, he walked away.

Close to 7 a.m., I received a call to a local bar for a report of a burglary. The break-in was from a backdoor which was newly installed that same day. The framing was pulled loose and the white caulk around the frame was smeared on the door. Remembering the white substance on Tommy's hands, it didn't take much common sense to connect the two. After asking the bar owner who did the replacement, he said, "Benny Tucker," a local contractor, and "Tommy was his helper," confirming my suspicion.

The following 4 p.m. to midnight shift, we confronted Tommy with what I knew. Instead of the hassle of an arrest and a court case that would more than likely be thrown out, we settled for information. He told us about a guy who was suspected of being the second largest supplier of heroin in the city hiding out in the project, and gave us a description of the car and the person in question.

During the week, we periodically checked the project parking lots and at the end of that week, we swung through the Fillmore Place parking lot and saw the car. It was winter and we could see the exhaust, so we knew the car was running. There was a black male sitting in the driver's seat and another approaching from a project building. I approached the driver's side with my revolver in hand and Jesse was on the passenger side. After getting the driver out of the car we talked to both of them about what we knew.

Realizing we knew about him hiding out in the project, he took a roll of hundred dollar bills large enough to choke a horse from his pocket and said, "Here's thirty five hundred. It's yours if you don't take me in."

Jesse replied, "Thanks for giving me something to charge you with asshole."

After placing them in the wagon, Jesse drove the wagon and I drove the defendant's car to the district. While driving, I happen to put my hand down along-side the bucket-seat and felt a gun. At the district, we went directly to the detective division on the second floor. After running the serial number of the revolver through N.C.I.C., it was discovered the revolver belonged to a Brinks armored car driver. They were delivering money to a large furniture store at Broad and Washington Street in South Philadelphia and were held up. Several people in the store at the time were shot during the incident. An elderly Jewish couple shopping in the store at the time became witnesses, and several days later, they were found murdered in their home in the Northeast section of the city. There was no clue as to who the perpetrators were, and the case was at a dead-end for Major Crimes Unit. The revolver was the first clue to the case, and night-command was notified. After he arrived, Jesse and I related the circumstances of the arrest.

When he asked about the gun I found, I told them the full story. The command had a short conference out of listening range, and Jesse and I wondered what was being said. The night command officer asked us to write out the story and had us sign separate arrest reports. There was an old detective in the unit by the name of Bill Sloss. Walking by us he quietly said, "Kid, don't sign anything that doesn't have a story attached."

Thinking he was overly cautious, we didn't listen and signed the papers. After signing, we were excused for the rest of the tour with a pat on the back, and a job well done.

The following day after reporting in, we were told by the corporal we were wanted upstairs in the detective division. Handing us a copy of the report attached to our signatures, I immediately realized the old detective was right. Finding the gun was totally illegal without a search warrant, and the story attached was something no one would have believed. There was no mention about the bribe at all. I looked at Jesse with skepticism and he looked at me. I said, "Hey dude, this is perjury, pure perjury. We put ourselves in the hot seat."

Fortunately, the defendants waived a preliminary hearing at the district, opting to go directly to Common Pleas Court. We received court notices a week later to appear on a Tuesday, and every day that passed preceding it, I became more uncomfortable dreading its arrival.

On the Sunday before the case we were working the day shift. At roll call Jesse was smiling, not acting at all like he was worried. I said, "What the fuck are you so happy about? We better get our testimony together before Tuesday."

"Didn't you see the newspaper today?" he replied.

"No. Why?"

"The guys we locked up were shot to death by two white guys in a bar on Susquehanna Avenue yesterday."

After he said it, a feeling of great relief went through my mind. The bar where the homicide took place was in a completely black neighborhood, so the perpetrators of the shooting being white, lent to the reason we were offered the $3,500. It was obviously a hit which confirmed the important position of both victims.

We learned a great lesson that day, and that was to never sign anything that doesn't have a story attached. To think you can always trust command depends on political pressure that sometimes becomes an over-riding factor.

CHAPTER 9

The Muslims

As time went on, we began to have unofficial complaints of what we called at the time "Jailhouse Muslims." These were people who were incarcerated for one offense or another, and while in prison, adopted the religion.

Several were from the neighborhood prior to being arrested and we were told they were robbing drug dealers, recruiting them to work by intimidation. It was said by several people who were there at the time, they would barge into a drug house brandishing guns and threaten the occupants by sticking guns in the wives or children's mouth. They were also extorting protection money from several merchants. We were familiar with who they were, but without a formal complaint, our hands were tied. We realized it would only be a matter of time before they went too far and someone would get killed, and it seemed the longer it went on, the bolder they became. There were several local store robberies we could attribute to them to, but they were statements from people who didn't want to make an official complaint.

On a 4 p.m. to midnight shift one Friday evening, for some reason Jesse and I were separated and he was working a neighboring car. Around

8:30 p.m., there was a report of a holdup at a sizable men's clothing store just off Frankford Avenue. It was a Friday during the Christmas season with about twenty patrons individually robbed as well as the store cash-registers. The manager and assistant manager had been shotgun whipped and put in a closet. From the descriptions given by the victims, we realized they were the same people we were told who were terrorizing the neighborhood.

At that time, we carried what we referred to as a rogue's gallery of around fifty arrest photographs. I picked out around twenty to show to several victims with a few of the peoples pictures we suspected mixed in. Just as we figured, the six photos picked out of the twenty were the same people. After putting out the description on police radio, Jesse handled the rest of the assignment.

Around 11:30 p.m. while making a last minute check of the sector, I saw two of the perpetrators walking towards me on a darkened street. Calling for a backup, Jesse responded and we took them into custody. After being identified by the victims, they were formally charged.

Two of the people who were part of the group, would later be involved with the seven Hanafi Muslims murdered in a home in Washington, D.C., owned by a professional basketball player. They were incarcerated to a term in Holmesburg Prison for another offense, and while serving time waiting for a court case on the robbery charge, one decided to talk to the Feds. Several days later, he was found hanging in his cell with two butcher knives shoved up his rectum. It seemed as though prison wasn't exactly the safest place to be.

In 1969, the underground groups like the Black Panthers were also causing havoc. There was an incident in Cobb's Creek Park in West Philadelphia. A police park guard sergeant was shot to death in a guard house. I was on a bus detail that evening and was called to the scene. We were instructed that there might have been hand grenades with trip wires set in the park area. I personally did not come across any in our sweep, but there were several found throughout the park.

In 1970 there was a riot in Holmsburg Prison. It was at first about over-crowding conditions at the institution, but wound up to be a racial issue. That riot was put down rather quickly by the direction of the police commissioner, who called for every available police car in the division. Jesse and I upon arrival met at the front gate with other officers who responded to the call. Going in the front, gate we were told to face the crowd and go forward. Any inmate who didn't go back to their cell voluntarily was to be dealt with forcefully. There were quite a few inmates injured in the melee, and the bloody scenes were an indication of the severity of the violence. That riot would be dwarfed by another at the prison several years later. There were people arrested for this incident and given life terms. A couple who were involved were also involved in another riot in 1973.

In early 1973, Jesse and I were hearing rumblings about something stirring in Holmesburg Prison between two different factions. There was nothing definite, but in a conversation with Father Palumbo, the priest from Matter DeLarosa while assigned to a church event, I mentioned what I had heard. Several days later, there was a riot at the prison which claimed the life of the Warden and Deputy Warden, along with other inmates who were stabbed to death. In that riot, over a hundred prisoners took part, and many inmates as well as guards were severely injured by other inmates. The two leaders were serving a sentence of life in prison for the killing of a police sergeant and many other crimes.

We weren't on duty that day, but quite a few police in that section of the city were called to the prison. We were told, by other cops that were there, what took place. I quote a friend from a squad that was working the day shift who said, "Mayor Rizzo was on the scene and immediately took control. After gathering the police that answered the call around at the front gate he said, "After you walk into the yard, half of you go to the right and half go to the left. Face the crowd and go forward. I don't want to see anyone standing that doesn't go back into the building voluntarily."

The officer who related the story said, "I followed the crowd into the building, and happened to go into the kitchen area. The blood on the tile floor from inmates slashing each other was almost deep enough to cover the soles of my shoes, and the blood pool was wide enough to cover a good portion of the floor."

After I asked whether it was part racial he replied, "It was strictly racial."

Needless to say, the riot ended almost as quickly as it began. Later that month when I saw Father Palumbo again, he mentioned the conversation we had.

During the early seventies, Muslim Groups were becoming out of hand with aggressiveness in many parts of the city. A rookie cop assigned to the squad name Tommy Parker was working the Torresdale section of the district on a late 4 p.m. to midnight shift. He stopped to investigate an unoccupied auto parked on a street near a commuter train station.

As he was looking over the auto, he was shot by someone with a high-powered rifle, who was on the embankment where the railroad tracks are. The shot passed through his upper cheekbone and after blowing out the roof of his mouth, passed through his lower jaw, shattering it. The bullet then passed through his collarbone and exited his arm. He didn't die, but was critical at Nazareth Hospital. I happened to be off that night and Jesse knowing I had given blood on many occasions, called to tell me about it, and I immediately went to the hospital to give blood. I'm what they call a universal donor, O negative blood type. I can give blood to any other blood type.

It was later discovered the shooter and the other male on the hill were the owners of the car being investigated. They were Muslims going to attempt a jail-break from Holmsburg Prison of one of their group. One male was apprehended that night hiding among the weeds along the railroad tracks and the other escaped.

Tommy had to go through twenty five operations to get his face reconstructed, and never returned to the police department. Meeting him years later, he told me the shooter was arrested in California almost twenty five years after it happened.

* * *

Unrelated to the Muslim Crime, it wouldn't have been the first time I had given blood to a wounded police officer, or someone else who was in need.

Several years after arriving at the 15th, I was working the midnight to 8 a.m. tour stationed outside Frankford High School. There had been some sort of teacher's union dispute and the police were standing by in case of a problem.

Around 7:30 a.m. a call came out in the 7th District of an officer being shot, and shortly after, another call went out for O-negative Blood. I responded and quickly headed for Nazareth Hospital where the officer had been taken. Lying on the bed in the hospital giving blood in the adjacent room, I looked over and saw a Black Highway Patrol Officer named Devereaux doing the same.

The officer shot was answering a call of a burglary in progress at a doctor's residence. After entering the rear door of the home, one of the burglars was hiding behind the door and fired a shot, striking the officer in the neck. The perpetrator was gunned down by responding police officers and died on the front lawn of the residence.

Unfortunately, for the officer that was shot, even with all the immediate medical effort, he didn't make it, and died in the emergency room.

Several days later I was given the honor and privilege to stand at the head of the casket during his viewing. Some months after the burial, they named a playground in the northeast after him.

Targeting businesses for extortion and robberies were increasing, and it seemed to be an added way to extract money for the Muslim Organization. There was an increase of robberies to businesses that were open in the early or late hours of the day, and we patrolled the vulnerable businesses as often as possible.

One midnight to 8 a.m. shift when Dave Tulley was patrolling a dark side street off Torresdale Avenue, he happened upon a vehicle with four black male occupants and could tell by the exhaust the motor was running. Realizing they were in a position to watch a fast-food restaurant about to open, he was preparing to investigate. With his spotlight shining through the rear window of the car, he was about to walk up to the vehicle. Driving down Torresdale Avenue, I saw his spot light shining and pulled into the one way street in the opposite direction, blocking the vehicle he was about to investigate. Focusing my spotlight in the front window, the group in the car realizing they were in no position to get away, quickly gave up.

After placing them in the police wagon, the car was brought to the district. Four guns were retrieved from the vehicle and a ballistics test of one, confirmed it was involved in a homicide in another district. The continued investigation by a newly-assigned detective by the name of Kenny Curcio revealed three out of the four were identified from photos to be the holdup men we were looking for. In retrospect, it's lucky Jesse and I were patrolling when we saw Dave about to approach the car. If not, he may have been another victim of a homicide.

Most of the people belonging to the group were thugs before going to jail. Joining the Muslim organization was only a cover for protection while there, and some kept the façade after leaving for financial gain.

The continued group participation for some may have been earnest, but the majority were there to do what they didn't have guts to do alone. Most of them eventually shunned the suit and tie which Muslims adopt, eventually returning to crime supporting drug use or alcoholism.

Unfortunately, the drug culture had a devastating effect on the neighborhood, which hastened the departure of upscale businesses and longtime residents. The loss of jobs also exacerbated the situation. I've found through speaking with many people reliant on public welfare, that most of them lose self respect, and one of the biggest let downs for them is losing the dignity of being the provider.

There will always be people who take money used for a safety net, and convert it into a well padded hammock, but I firmly believe more people given the opportunity to work, would rather have a job. As generation, after generation receives public monies, the idea of working for a living becomes a moot point.

The public handout is only life sustaining, but the desire of luxuries continues, and most of the time the only recourse to make up that difference is through crime.

CHAPTER 10

Drug distribution

The departure of organized drug dealing through intimidation was soon taken over by a host of people filling in the void. The dealing in the project wasn't easy to enforce and through a few letters from Jesse and I, the Housing Authority adopted the position of evicting people from apartments where it went on. It forced suppliers to recruit people, often junkies, who would deal just to support their own habit. Other than that, girls usually turn to prostitution and shop-lifting, while men turn to burglary, robbery, or even male prostitution, anything to earn a few dollars.

In the lower end of the district, one center of distribution was a hangout at a fast food restaurant on Torresdale Avenue and Kinsey Street. There was an alley behind the houses on Kinsey Street with a fence blocking its entry from Torresdale Avenue. Standing on a small stool, we were able to view the side and front of the establishment from across the street without being detected. As cold weather was quickly becoming a factor, I decided to speak with the owner of a four-story Ribbon Factory across the street from the restaurant to see if he would allow us to use the building. From the second floor, we were able to observe what was going on much easier.

Through his generosity, we were able to gain a lot of information which led to quite a few arrests.

On occasion we would swoop down to roundup a group hanging out, and after taking them to the district, we would examine their arms for track marks. The visible marks were where multiple injections were made, and if we discovered they were juveniles, we would contact their parents.

Although I realized the lure of money for not making arrests was a factor with some police officers, there was an incident that occurred by a newly-assigned cop in the district. He had around five or six years in the department and the incident occurred by him unscrupulously using my name.

After taking a group of young people to the district, from the fast-food restaurant one 4 p.m. to midnight shift, I was in the operations-room making calls to parents while Jesse was getting more information from the group we brought in. In a few minutes, he entered the operations room and asked me to step outside. When I asked what the problem was, he told me to remove my nametag and listen to what one of the teenage girls had to say. She was an attractive sixteen-year-old who looked more mature than her age, and Jesse asked her to repeat to me what she told him.

She stated she had gone to a motel with one of the officers several times in return for not notifying her parents. When I asked who the officer was, she said my last name. Shocked, I looked at Jesse realizing why he told me to remove my nametag. I asked the girl when the officer was working, and she said he was working this shift. When I asked what number car he was in, she told me. Looking at Jesse, I couldn't believe what I was hearing. The cop whose first name was Leo was transferred from another district about a year and a half before. I didn't know why, but hearing what this teenager was saying, I assumed it too was for disciplinary reasons.

At my request, Jesse called police-radio to have him report to the district. I told Jesse when he arrives have him come to the roll-room.

It took him around ten minutes to get to the district and during the waiting time I was only getting more infuriated. To think another cop would do such a thing was without a doubt, the most vile act I ever heard of. Had it turned out differently, chances are my name could have been splashed all over the front page of the newspaper, and in my mind I envisioned the headline: *Officer takes sex for silence with teenager.*

The more I thought about it, the more my anger built up to a point I knew I was going to explode. I realized Jesse knew what I was thinking and came into the roll-room with Leo when he arrived. After taking a few steps into the room, I think Leo realized what was going to happen. His face turned red with embarrassment and I didn't give him time to think before punching him in the mouth. He hit the wall before falling to the floor and Jesse grabbed me trying to hold me back from slamming him again. The Corporal, realizing something was going on, told Chris, one of the men from the operations-room to follow him. They came into the room as Jesse was trying to hold me back from going after Leo again, and helped restrain me. Leo was semi-conscious and I think it was obvious the punch fractured his jaw.

After taking me into a small room off the hallway, Jesse and Chris stayed, while the Corporal went to the operations room to call for a police car to take Leo to the hospital. He then notified the district captain, and night command inspector about the incident.

After the captain arrived he asked me what happened. He knew Jesse and my record on the street warranted some further investigation of what took place and after asking me why it happened, I refused to talk.

When the night command inspector arrived, there was some discussion with the captain out of hearing range. I imagined the discussion was about whatever disciplinary action they were going to take, and I realized at the least, I would be charged with assault and battery.

After the discussion they took my revolver and escorted me upstairs to the detective division. After placing me in an interview room, they allowed Jesse to stand by with me. Realizing the seriousness of the charge and the obvious loss of my job, Jesse begged me to tell them what happened. I still refused to talk and in turn, told him not to say anything.

After several hours, they released me and told me I was on administrative leave and sent me home. Jesse called every day to see how I was doing, and every time he called, I was hoping for some kind of word one way or the other.

Finally after a few days, the captain came to my home. After returning my revolver he informed me I was to return to work the following day. When I asked about Leo possibly pressing charges, he replied there would be none against me, and Leo was no longer in the district. I really never knew for sure what was resolved, but I believe it was a compromise. Not being arrested for the assault, for him not being prosecuted for what he had done. I too, think with Jesse and my record of police work on the street, was probably a major factor in that decision. I found out later Leo resigned from the force and I never saw him again.

Like the classmates who were arrested in the police academy, integrity's a quality that has to already be within a person who decides to become a cop or it doesn't exist at all, and there's no way to pre-judge that in a person.

It was obvious the effect of drugs on our society had taken on a completely different revision of narcotic users as we previously knew it. They were no longer back alley adult users. This infection was taking hold of the younger generation and would set the stage for expanding drug use in schools, some as low as seventh and eighth graders. We were also instrumental in capturing a few juvenile runaways and returning them home. The sad part about it was the fact we would see the same people eventually standing outside the methadone program on Paul Street in the early morning hours. The satisfaction came when some of them we knew, actually cleaned up their act, and thanked us for what we had done.

In fact, it's now 40 years later, and one of the people who cleaned up their act saw my name recently on Facebook. After she asked whether I was the person who worked with Jesse, I confirmed that fact. After some conversation, she made a statement that made me feel our efforts weren't completely in vain.

Her statement was, "When you two and Galliano were working, every junkie who was dealing was afraid to come out on the street." After bringing me abreast of what happened to some of the people we used to deal with, she said and I quote, "Most of the people we knew were already dead. Probably from that shit we used to put in our bodies. We used to think you guys were the enemy, but the truth is, the motherfucker's that was selling us that shit were."

That conversation took me back years when the Jess and I were young and truly believed in our cause. After signing off, I spent the rest of the evening reminiscing about some of the contacts we had with most of the people she spoke about. The strange part, I remembered their faces and the circumstances that brought us together as though it happened yesterday.

One of the problems hampering the enforcement of drug use was the ease in which it was being purchased. Other than radio calls unassociated, we spent as much time as possible patrolling the areas where it was suspected of being sold. The dealers were increasingly finding ways to do it that took us to the edge of legality making arrests.

Some of the innovative ways to avoid detection was a loose brick in a wall several buildings away from where the dealer would take the money.

One arrest we made was for a dealer who concreted the bottom of a sewer on the northwest corner of Mulberry and Orthodox Street. He saved only a small opening, allowing rain water to enter the sewer system. He would take the money several houses away and the car with the purchaser would pull up to the corner. The person standing in the sewer transacted the sale by the driver opening the car door without leaving the vehicle. Without an informant, we would have probably never known about it.

Another case was a car stop in the project. Through an informant, we were able to get a description of a car with a white male and a black male, suppliers from another section of the city. We saw the car speeding through the project on the 4 p.m. to midnight shift one warm summer evening and pulled it over. Approaching the driver's side, I observed through the open window on the floor of the passenger side, a stack of money orders extending from an open brown paper bag. After taking them into custody, I drove the car to the district. We brought them and the money orders to the detective division, where they discovered the serial numbers matched money orders taken in an armed robbery of a grocery store that same day in a different district.

The initial purpose for stopping the car was for narcotics, and we discovered several boxes of small heroin bags and a small scale in the trunk, so we knew we were on the right path.

Sitting in the driver's seat at the district, I was tapping the horn section of the steering wheel with the car keys, wondering where the drugs were hidden. Suddenly, the center piece of the steering wheel moved. Lifting the cap of the horn, the heroin was inside the column. Little did I realize the inspector of the division happened to be standing next to the vehicle when I discovered it and asked, "Do you have a warrant for that?"

"No, Inspector," I replied, telling him the probable cause behind taking them into custody.

Thinking it wouldn't be a problem, we settled for the arrest as it was. When the case went to court, it was thrown out due to not having a warrant for the heroin search. We found out later there was some political consideration given because of a connection with the white occupant. It was obvious it wasn't the first time he was allowed to go free. He had eleven prior arrests for various offences without serving any time.

Jesse and I discussed many times the legality of taking someone down for heroin without really knowing what the substance was before the chemical analysis, but seeing the effects of drugs, we always felt the end justified the means for arresting dealers.

Jesse had been divorced for quite some time, and due to financial commitments, hadn't had a chance to get a social life. There was a beautiful exceptionally well-built light skinned black girl by the nickname of "Bunny" living on our sector. It was summer and she always dressed in a very short one-piece terrycloth hot-pants outfit. When she saw us parked, she would pass our vehicle and throw Jesse a wide smile, sometimes stopping to chat. I chided him about not making a date with her and told him I was willing to finance his adventure. He finally cracked when I got tired of their conversations about going out without a definite commitment and said, "If you don't pull that, you're not much of a man."

He finally broke down and made the date. After several dates for some reason, she began to shun us.

Several weeks later, we were informed of a shipment of heroin coming into the district from the Germantown section of the city, and given the names and make of car that would be delivering it.

The quickest way to the district from that end of the city was coming over Adams Avenue, a wide thoroughfare, so we positioned ourselves at the entrance of a cemetery just east of the Roosevelt Blvd. When we observed the car during a day-work tour, we pulled it over. The passenger appeared to bend down as we walked up to the vehicle and as we were standing next to it, the operator jumped out of the car. In a loud tone he yelled to the passenger, "What the fuck did you just throw under my seat?"

"If it's your vehicle, whatever it is, you own it," I said as I walked toward them.

His reply was, "Fuck that shit! All I'm doing is giving this mother fucker a ride. I'll get whatever he put there."

Reaching under the seat, he retrieved 4 bundles of heroin (which amounts to 100 small packets) and handed them to me. After taking them into custody, we made the arrest.

Several days later we were in the district when the Corporal said, "Jesse, you have a phone call in the operations room."

"Who is it?" he replied.

"It's an Assistant D.A."

Picking up the phone, Jesse seemed to be fumbling for words with whoever he was speaking to, so I stopped to listen. After he hung up I asked, "What was that about?"

With a bewildered look he replied, "He asked me if I always shit where I eat."

Looking puzzled by his remark I asked, "Who, the Assistant District Attorney? What the hell did he mean by that?"

"He said the guy we locked up for the heroin on Adams Avenue was Bunny's brother."

There were other narcotics arrests to numerous to mention, but informants were always the prime source of our success.

CHAPTER 11

Reshuffling the deck

In 1972 or 1973, the Philadelphia Police Department went through a major change. All Sergeants, Lieutenants and Captains were transferred to different districts. I didn't know for sure, but I believe it was around the same time New York was experiencing the corruption within the ranks of their narcotics and uniform divisions. Maybe it was a preventive measure in Philadelphia, of that I wasn't sure.

    I do know of one incident published in the newspaper we were familiar with that happened in the upper end of our district. With Jesse and me knowing some of the people involved in drugs, we were given second hand information about it that we believed to be accurate. The newspaper article was about a home being served with a search warrant by a narcotics team, and allegedly a trash-bag full of money disappearing. A parent to of one of the officers involved was a high-ranking member in the department, and the officers were given the opportunity to resign. We always believed the case was put to rest for obvious reasons. Several years later, one of the officers involved opened several bars in and around Philadelphia.

It seemed as though Jesse and I were making better arrests in uniform than the plain clothes narcotics unit, which wasn't supposed to be. In fact, we were approached one day when we took an arrest to Narcotics and the lieutenant said, "You guys are making us look bad up there. Why don't you lighten up and share the information you're getting? As a matter of fact, why don't you transfer here?"

I didn't trust the statement because we knew they could have done what we were able to do without a problem. The underlying meaning without saying it; was about money. We had heard many stories from not only junkies, but street dealers verifying that fact.

With the transfers, it began to become challenging with the new sergeant. Within several weeks of his arrival, he confronted Jesse and I with the possibility of getting gratuities from different sources he thought we may have been getting. Known numbers people, card games, clubs or bars operating illegally, and hinted around drug dealers. The conversation ended with me telling him, "We don't have any clubs on our sector, and I wouldn't put myself or my job in jeopardy by doing that."

Walking away I mentioned to Jesse, "I think our ability to police effectively is short lived."

His reply was optimistic saying, "I don't think so."

"Well, time will tell," I replied.

There was an Italian Club on our sector, a remnant of when the neighborhood was predominant with Italian and Ukrainian immigrants. It hadn't been in continuous use for many years, but on rare occasions would host a Christmas party or wedding reception. One midnight to 8 a.m. shift a call came out of a fight on the street in front of the club. Before we arrived

I told Jesse, "I'll bet the sergeant gets there before us and thinks we're hiding something from him."

Pulling up to the location, I was spot on. The fight had already been taken care of but the sergeant waved for us to join him. After approaching him he said, "I thought you told me there wasn't any clubs on your sector?"

"Sergeant, that club hasn't been open continuously for years. In fact, I forgot about it until now," I replied.

As we walked back to our vehicle I mentioned to Jesse, "This isn't the end of this. He thinks we're lying."

From that day forward, we were assigned every detail away from the district that came down the pike. Our vehicle was reassigned to other squad members, many of them recent arrivals from other districts. It became bad enough, I eventually mentioned to Jesse I was volunteering to take the detail in Southwest Philadelphia, a foot beat in the 30th and Tasker Public Housing Project. The detail was from mid May to just after Labor Day in September. It was at least an hour from my residence, and about twenty more miles, but the aggravation of not working under those circumstances was a benefit.

At almost the same time, Jesse was offered a plainclothes assignment to work the vice-squad in center city, and as it turned out, we were both able to escape the unprovoked hostility of the sergeant for several months.

* * *

Returning to the district wasn't as bad as it had been, but occasionally we would be assigned other cars and different details. I did notice that in our absence, there was a definite change in attitude of the lower end squad members, and prior to roll-call one 4 p.m. to midnight shift I stood up in front of the squad. Raising hell with the members, I made the famous statement, "We're like vegetables in a pot; the only difference is the spoon that stirs us up. When it's gone, we'll still be here to deal with each other." I think it sunk in, but the damage was already obvious.

The inspector of Northeast Division saw Jesse and I in the hallway one day and asked, "What's with you two? You always led the division with felony arrests?"

In mild conversation, I mentioned Jesse and I not working our usual assignment. Looking confused at my statement we parted. The next day we were reassigned 1501 wagon and being put on different details came to an end. Whatever was said remained a mystery, but the pressure of taking gratuities for the sergeant continued.

There was a church at Mulberry and Meadow Street whose pastor came to the district to file a complaint against Jesse and me. The complaint was about the harassment of the pastor's twenty-year-old son. After the sergeant had taken the complaint, he summoned us to the district. After some conversation, he referred the complaint to the lieutenant. Little did we know at the time, the complaint was initiated by the sergeant.

At a meeting in the captain's office between the pastor, the sergeant and lieutenant, we listened to the pastor's complaint. After his statement, the captain asked if we had anything to say. I spoke up telling him the pastor's son was a junkie and one of our biggest informants. The captain looked at the pastor for a response but instead the pastor cast a glance at the sergeant. When he did, it became obvious to me where the complaint originated, and as time passed, we discovered I was spot on with my suspicion.

After the meeting, the captain asked Jesse and I to remain. Alone in his office he asked, "What's with you guys. You were always go getters? And you Bishop, you've been taking a lot of sick time lately. What gives?"

"Captain, I've been having a few medical problems and I've been going to the Police Clinic for treatment."

"So what's the story?" he asked.

"I had a spike in my blood pressure, and after all the tests came out negative for anything physical, they said it was due to stress and gave me a prescription. It seems to be working, so I'm good to go."

"Is it problems at home or on the job?" he bluntly asked.

I didn't want to say, so I blew the question off. I think by doing that and the meeting we just had, he pretty much narrowed it down where the trouble was coming from. Whatever transpired between him the lieutenant and the sergeant after that was unknown, but things began to fall back to normal.

Occasionally the sergeant would badger us about gratuities but after a time, finally realizing we weren't going to be a part of that, gave up asking. It remained that way until he was transferred from the district.

After he left, things began to return to normal. Our informants kept giving us information but due to their narcotic addiction would still do burglaries. One midnight to 8 a.m. shift, a call came out of a robbery by point of gun. From the description, we pretty much knew it was Floyd Williamson, one of our best informants. We went to the residence of his girlfriend where we knew he occasionally stayed, but before we could get there, a call came out of a shooting and a hospital case at a vacant property close by. After arriving, we discovered Floyd was shot by another cop, a rookie newly-assigned to the district. As a result we had to rebuild our base of informants, and the reverend's son once again, took up the slack.

Not long after that incident, we were assisting policeman Galliano serve a warrant on the 4 p.m. to midnight shift at a three-story Victorian home on Tackawanna Street. An informant of ours made a narcotics buy at the house at our request, and returned to where we were waiting. He informed us there were several known dealers and four people – six total – inside the residence.

I asked, "Are you sure there's only six, and are they locals?"

"Two are, but the others aren't. One I know is from North Philly, his name is Garfield. I didn't see anyone else and I didn't hear anyone upstairs so I guess that's all."

"Did they say anything to you?" Jesse asked.

"No. They just sort of looked at me like they didn't want me to know they were there."

"What did you do then?" I asked.

"I made the buy and left. I can tell you this, two of them had guns."

After the conversation, we felt it necessary to ask for another backup unit. After the backup arrived, we served the warrant. With the backup unit covering the rear of the property, Galliano, Jesse and I went to the front door. With one swing of the sledgehammer the door flew open and we made a quick entry with guns drawn. The two occupants we knew who lived in the house, as well as three others we didn't know, quickly gave up. We could hear noise upstairs of someone moving around, and with one person not accounted for we assumed it was that person.

After handcuffing them together, we put them in the police wagon. Galliano called to the person we heard upstairs to come down but got no reply. Cautiously climbing the stairs, we began to slowly make our way down the darkened hall carefully searching each room. Most Victorian homes before air conditioning had almost floor to ceiling windows, and multiple doors connecting each room. In warm days, they would be opened to allow outside air to circulate freely. As it was winter, the second floor was cold obviously from an open window. Searching room-to-room, Galliano stepped into a room to check a closet. I was still in the hall and through the space on the hinge side of the door I was able to see a person standing behind it. He appeared to be holding a shotgun and it looked as though he was raising it to fire the weapon.

I threw my weight against the door as hard as I could, and the door, striking the person, sent him headlong across the room and through an open window. Quickly entering the room, I looked out and saw the person sprawled out on top of a large evergreen bush. Luckily it broke his fall, and the officers covering the rear of the property quickly took him into custody. The reason he was reluctant to give up, he was wanted for a homicide that took place in another district.

CHAPTER 12

Youths

It never ceased to amaze me why most young black people in the community, looked on drug dealers as someone to be respected rather than blight on the neighborhood. Being young and easily influenced by flashy clothes, Mister-T starter-sets, and pockets full of cash from street dealers, was probably enough incentive to disregard any moral upbringing. Some street dealers were as young as thirteen.

The shame of it; there were plenty of people we encountered with athletic talent as well as other attributes in the art and building skills, that could have gone farther had it not been for drugs.

One case was a concrete contractor named Arthur Moses. Arthur was in his mid-thirties and probably the best concrete porch and step contractor in Frankford. I would venture to say, he probably did 75% of the ones that were done. Getting hooked on heroin that late in life was an anomaly, but for whatever reason that was the case, and it left his family literally stranded financially.

A wife with several young children too proud to take public welfare was ethically correct, but trying to make a living salvaging scrap metal and newspapers on trash night wasn't filling the gap. The law in Philadelphia at the time was picking trash during the hours of dark was illegal. Jesse and I would see her driving an old beat-up station-wagon with her two preteen boys Lamont and Mario, picking up trash in the early morning hours. It didn't take much intelligence to figure out the kids being deprived of sleep, would affect their attention in school. Fortunately, with Jesse and I helping on occasion by telling her where things of value might be, it made her burden a little lighter.

In a conversation with her one morning, I reminded her about an outside block party where she was barbecuing the event. She said she was able to earn a few dollars to supplement her income that day. After putting our heads together, Jess and me had an idea to solicit a bar owner to allow her to serve takeout meals at his establishment on Friday and Saturday nights. He agreed and she no longer had to face an uncertain future by picking through trash.

There are a few cops like myself who take particular interest in a youth, and I knew of one other who lived in the Frankford area. I don't recall his name but remember he worked in the 2nd District. He took under his wing a youth who excelled in football. Upon graduating from Frankford High School, he received a full scholarship to a college I fail to remember the name of. While home on summer vacation he got involved with another youth and wound up killing the person, and was sentenced to life in prison.

That was one of the unfortunate youths who returned to the neighborhood he tried so desperately to escape from.

I took a personal interest in Lamont, and while he was in high school, I took him and sometimes Mario along with several other neighborhood youths after school to earn a few dollars. At the time, I was working as a contractor for a savings and loan office and other businesses on my beat.

Fortunately, Lamont being the more intelligent of the two was able to acquire the grades to remain in school and excel in football. However, before graduating, he got involved with stealing auto parts and was arrested. Personally knowing his background, I petitioned the judge in Juvenile Court to have him sent to Glenn Mills instead of Shall Cross, the better of the two juvenile institutions. While there, he excelled in football once again and attained a free scholarship to a technical college. By the request of his mother, I was honored to be his parent representative at the football awards banquet. After being released, he began working at construction for a few years, but the lure of big money returned. This time, he became involved in the drug trade with the son of a reputable jeweler, and being an adult cost him severely. He spent the next few years in prison. After his release, we had a conversation. I asked him what he felt like doing and he decided to pursue a cooking career. He straightened out his life and became a successful owner of a catering service, catering some of the professional Philadelphia baseball team events.

Several other encounters with teens in the neighborhood would also be a determining factor of how they grew up. A few times when we caught one of them wrong, we would take them home to a parent who we knew would dispense harsher justice than a court system. Long after Jesse and I went our different ways, I maintained that same policy.

On one occasion, I caught several youths trying to break into a car. Instead of arresting them, knowing the parents, I knew they would deal out a better punishment. Taking one of them home to a single mother in the project was all that was necessary. After knocking on the door Mrs. Thompson opened it and asked, "Hi Bishop! What's going on?"

"I caught your son and Sledgy," *a nickname for another youth,* "trying to break into a car."

A big woman, she reached around me grabbing her son by the collar pulling him into the house. After striking him a few times, she threw him down on the couch and pounced on him, proceeding to pound the hell out of him. In her fit of rage she yelled, "Nigger, I brought you into this world and I'll take your fuckin' ass out. I work my ass off for you, and that's the best you can return your love." After a few more slaps she thanked me and I left.

That same kid turned out to be a great running back for Frankford High School winning a full scholarship to a University. Before I retired, he saw me on the beat and we had a great conversation. He reminded me of that evening and thanked me for the outcome.

While I'm on the subject, another incident comes to mind. As I mentioned, I had several youths working with me fixing houses for a Savings and Loan Office after school. Two of them lived in the project with their mother, another brother, and several sisters. Eleanor, their mother, was a conscientious person doing the best she could under a stressful circumstance.

What most people don't realize who aren't familiar with this type of environment, it's for the most part violent. Conscientious parents like Eleanor can only guide children when they're at home, but there are times when they can't control outside influences. She had a young son at the age of 16 who was shot to death by another youth.

She had another son, Wayne, who worked for me after school. He showed promise with his boxing ability and I financed him when he joined Joe Frazier's Gym, a professional prize fighter. While still in high school, he had a confrontation with an adult living in the project who threatened him for some reason. A fight ensued and Wayne struck him. The attacker fell to the ground striking his head against the curb, and however contact was made, he died.

There was no immediate arrest, because it happened at night without witnesses. Wayne called me at home to tell me what took place, and asked what he should do. I told him not to say anything and assured him I would speak with someone. I knew the deceased to be a neighborhood tough and a drug dealer with a lengthy arrest record, and the next day I called the captain of the Homicide Unit. After explaining the situation, there was no more said about the incident.

Today, he, like the rest of the family no longer live in the project and are doing very well.

There is one aspect of living in a neighborhood like that. It seems if you can get a kid past the age of 20, chances are, they'll succeed in life. I realize that first hand, I came from a neighborhood like that, and saw many of my friends defeated by that sort of environment.

I can recall a community meeting I attended at the captain's request. The meeting was held in a local church with several prominent members of the community, and after the meeting two of them, approached me. They had heard I was taking several youths to work with me in the evening hours. One of them suggested I run for some sort of community organizer the people in the area would endorse. To their surprise, I laughed at the comment.

After asking me why I thought the statement was humorous I replied. "Everyone realizes what's plaguing the neighborhood; vacant houses that aren't boarded up, trash strewn lots, abandon autos that have been there for months at a time. These things are reported weekly by the police department; it's called a Sunday survey. Drugs are being sold practically with official sanction, by no one complaining to the councilmen representing the area. They always show up before the election to make promises, but no one holds their feet to the fire after. That's why I laughed."

After looking at one another, they realized I was right, and didn't pursue the conversation any further.

Part of policing is balancing the crime against whatever can be learned from the perpetrator. It isn't an all black and white issue; there is a gray area to be used at a cop's discretion. One incident happened not long after I was assigned the 15th. Working the midnight to 8 a.m. shift one Thanksgiving morning around 3:30 a.m., I was cruising the 1600 block of Church Street, when suddenly I saw a head duck down behind a parked auto. There were only a few houses at the far end of the street and a cemetery wall along the parking lane. There were parking meters on that side of the street and I stopped my vehicle short of where I saw the person. Without closing the car door, I walked past where I believed the person was hiding. Focusing on the police car, the person turned to make his escape in my direction. After handcuffing him, I walked him to my vehicle. Taking his identification I saw he was a high school kid, and looking at his dilated pupils, I realized he was strung out on drugs. He had been rifling the parking meters for coins with a large screwdriver, and had already broken into 8 or 10 along the street. After radioing for a police wagon, I took him to the detective division.

He was 17 and still considered a juvenile, but was willing to give me information he thought would negotiate his release.

At the time there were literally hundreds of autos being stolen in the immediate tri-state area and Frankford was one of the heaviest hit.

Throughout the lower end there was an abundance of single-unit parking garages. This was due to a law in the late twenties and early thirties that required automobile owners to have their cars parked in a driveway or garaged from midnight to 6 a.m. Most row homes didn't have either, so some people being entrepreneurs, built rows of garages wherever they could find open lots.

The youth said he knew one section nearby being used as a chop shop - *the street definition for breaking down stolen auto's into different components to sell.* Some autos were left intact, only altered to disguise their origin and shipped to different cities or states for resale. When I asked where the garages were, he informed me they were behind the row houses and corner store on the southwest corner of Torresdale and Margaret Street.

Taking him upstairs to Northeast Detectives, he repeated his information to Detective Curcio, and he in turn related it to his lieutenant, a detective by the name of Costellano. After placing the youth in a holding-room, Detective Lieutenant, Detective Curcio and I went to the location. Trying the garage doors without success, I took the screwdriver I confiscated from the youth and loosened a door hinge. Peering in with my flashlight, to my surprise, the kid was right. After replacing the hinge, we returned to Detective Headquarters.

After securing a warrant, we returned to the scene. Whoever was operating the car theft ring rented six garages and took the partition walls out to make one long garage. We found three vehicles that were reported stolen within the last several days, and two were partially stripped. Detective Curcio found a stack of about 30 license plates, and in tracing them, discovered they were from recently stolen autos.

After calling Major Crimes to the scene, they found paperwork from several local garages as well as garages throughout the city and suburbs who ordered parts. The FBI was brought into the case and before the investigation was over, it was discovered the auto theft ring operated as far north as Boston, as far south as North Carolina, and as far west as Ohio. Needless to say, I let the kid walk with a warning.

One of the funniest parts of this story, the captain of a North Philadelphia police district was arrested for driving a stolen Ford Thunderbird.

CHAPTER 13

Pet peeves

Some people you deal with as a cop can be dealt with reasonably, while others only know one avenue, a force equal or slightly above their aggressiveness. Low educational levels and leniency of the court system must take an equal share of the failure as part of that roll, and it's beyond reason to deal rationally with someone who fits that category.

For example, working with Iron Mike one Christmas morning, we were just leaving the police garage at 26th and Master Street where it was located at the time. A radio call came out of a shooting and a hospital case in the same block we were in. Quickly pulling to the curb, we ran up the front steps with guns drawn. The storm door was closed but the front door was open, and we could see a person who looked to be in his late twenties or early thirties sitting on the sofa in the dimly-lit living room drinking a bottle of beer. He waived for us to come in and as we entered, I noticed a body lying face down next to the Christmas tree. After turning him over, the victim looked to be in his early or mid-twenties. I felt for a pulse then raised his eyelid, but there was no sign of life. After telling the person sitting on the couch the victim was dead, I asked who the person was and what happened. The person sitting on the sofa drinking a beer seemed to be devoid of any feeling for the victim and stated, "That's my brother. I capped that motherfucker."

"Well he's dead. Why'd you shoot him?"

He annoyingly replied, "I kept telling him not to run my sons train set backwards, he'd break it before the boy had a chance to play with it. He wouldn't listen, so I got my gun and capped that motherfucker," raising his bottle of beer as a salute to what he had done.

After a sector car, police wagon and sergeant arrived, Mike and I left. Arriving at Homicide Headquarters, we gave our statements as to what we knew. Looking at the shooters background and arrest record, he only went to the 8th grade, and had twelve prior arrests of varying charges, most of which were drug related.

Case in point: you can't deal rationally with that sort of mentality.

As I pointed out earlier, cops like any person, have pet peeves, and mine was older people being injured when they became targets of robberies. I also had no patience for people who abused children.

One case happened when I was detailed to the 18th District in West Philadelphia. I was at a school crossing for an elementary school when a young kid about the age of eight or nine approached. I was about to help him across the street, when he suddenly turned and sat down on a set of steps and began to cry. I asked, "What's wrong, didn't you get your homework done?"

After a few minutes he wiped his eyes replying, "No."

I asked again what was upsetting him and he reluctantly told me he was worried about his sister. When I asked what he meant, he said she was chained up in the basement of his house. I was shocked at his answer and asked how old she was. He said he didn't know, but told me she never went to school anymore then began to cry again. When I asked if he was making the story up he assured me it was the truth.

After calling for the sergeant, I related the boy's story. The sergeant took the boy in his car to show him where he lived, and I followed.

After knocking on the front door, a man who appeared to be in his late thirties opened it. When he saw the boy he became angry and said, "What the hell did my son do?"

The sergeant replied, "He didn't do anything wrong. He told us he has a sister chained up in the basement. Do you mind if we look?"

The look on the resident's face told me he was shocked by the knowledge the sergeant had, and tried closing the door. Quickly responding, I put my foot in the door and shoved it open, knocking him to the floor. He began to yell about not having a search warrant, but I was determined to look in the basement in spite of his comments. With the boy guiding us through the trash-strewn disheveled house, we got to the basement door. When the owner attempted again to get between me and opening the basement door, I shoved him out of the way. After opening the door and turning the basement light on, in the dimness of the basement, I saw what looked like an animal chained to the railing at the bottom of the steps, curled up lying on what looked like an old coat. Suddenly, it lifted its head to look at me, and I realized the boy was right, it was a human. The owner attempted to get between me again from going downstairs, but I gave him a shove that sent him headlong to the basement floor. Getting ready to go after him again, the sergeant had to restrain me until I finally calmed down.

After contacting Human Services and Juvenile Aid, I left the scene.

Later when I filed my report as to what happened, I asked the Juvenile Aid Officer about the girl. I was told she was nine-years-old and in poor physical health, something I already surmised. She had been chained to the same railing for almost two months being fed from a dog food bowl. When

I asked how long she was truant from school, the Juvenile Aid Officer stated she hadn't been there since the end of last semester.

I asked, "Why didn't the school inquire about her not attending?"

"The school assumed she went to live with another parent or guardian," the Juvenile Aid Officer replied.

When I asked what the outcome will be, I was told both children would be sent to live with their grandmother.

Case in point: although cops should maintain their composure, they're still human, and sometimes emotions overwhelming a situation cause a response that's spontaneous.

Cops aren't the only ones guilty of emotion or favoritism; it also exists in some judges and lawyers too.

Jesse and I were working the police wagon one hot summer evening and were answering a radio call of a silent alarm at a factory. While we were checking the building, a call came out of a rape in progress at a house on a small street just around the corner. Choosing to run to the location, I ran up the steps to the front porch, and Jesse ran down the side alley to the rear of the residence. The front door was open and as I reached for the handle of the screen door, I observed a male pulling up his trousers standing over a girl lying on the floor between the living room and dining room. Quickly looking in my direction, he ran toward the back door. By that time, Jesse was in the backyard and captured the suspect as he was making his exit. He was identified by the complainant as the one who raped her and we placed him in the wagon. After being booked, he was sent to central cell where he was processed.

Several weeks later we had a court appearance for the case, and after testifying the defendant was released on probation. The judge had to have seen his lengthy arrest record including one for child abuse, and normally after the person is found guilty the judge makes the sentence according to what they see in the persons background file.

The defendant also had several priors for narcotics arrests, a burglary charge, and several for receiving stolen property. To my personal knowledge, the same judge demonstrated partiality against the police several times in the past as if it was personal. A judge's courtroom is their domain and a protest by me to the Assistant District Attorney was useless.

Several weeks later, I arrested the same person for assaulting a nine-year-old girl. Thankfully, that case didn't go before the same judge so I was satisfied. The same female judge who allowed the rapist to go free the first time, was running for a seat on the State Supreme Court and while off duty, I actively campaigned against her appointment. Fortunately, she didn't make it.

Several months later, I heard she was the victim of a purse snatch in center city. I'd be willing to bet if the person was caught, she wouldn't have been so lenient.

Jesse and I spent many days in various courtrooms both in Common Pleas at city hall, and the Juvenile and Domestic Court located at 1801 Vine Street. As I pointed out, a Judge's courtroom is their domain, and on several occasions a judge being familiar with us, wouldn't allow a defense attorney do what they call badgering. That's asking the same question over and over phrasing it differently.

I had an occasion to have a court case involving an adult who was arrested with several juveniles for a strong-arm robbery. After I took the stand, the judge, saw there were other people involved, and leaned toward me asking what the case was about. After relating the defendant was the leader of the group of juveniles, the judge allowed very few questions from the defense. Wanting to make an example of the defendant, he gave him a sentence of 18 to 23 months in the House of Correction.

On that same case in Juvenile Court, the judge was an African American woman. The defense for the three youths was asking many questions and the judge who knew me from prior cases, saw my frustration. She stopped the defense and asked what was on my mind, something unusual for the demeanor of the court. The defense attorney began to protest, when the judge shut his protest down. After giving him a stern look, she asked me to continue. I related to the judge, "I assume we're all here to try and keep these kids from eventually winding up in Common Pleas Court; what good does it do to debate legality?"

The judge, in agreement, stopped the testimony and rendered the case accordingly. Jesse and I had many cases in front of the same judge and Juanita proved herself to be one of the better judges we encountered.

CHAPTER 14

Domestic disturbances

Jesse and I had many conversations over the 8 years we were together covering a variety of subjects. Some tales were on the humorous side about how we acted as rookies, and one of the stories he told me was about the first parking ticket he wrote. Apparently, he was called to a location and while writing the ticket, the owner of the vehicle arrived. He began to give Jesse a hard time verbally as he got into his auto. Before Jesse was finished the ticket, the driver started the car and put it in gear. Jesse nonchalantly unsnapped his holster and looked at the man. It not only ended the verbal assault, the guy politely took the ticket.

    I also had a situation that proved embarrassing. On a midnight to 8 a.m. shift there was a report of a shooting and a hospital case at the bar at Frankford and Unity Streets. It turned out to be a homicide by gunshot and after leaving the bar, I patrolled the area looking for the suspect. Driving through the bus terminal at Bridge Street, I saw a person fitting the description going up the stairs to the elevated train platform. Attempting to pull the police car out of the bus platform lanes, I struck a metal pole. Running up the El stairs to the platform, I discovered that the person was gone.

In those days, there was a director of safety who would hear your reason for the accident, and upon your testimony, would render his judgment accordingly. The hearings took place at the Police Administration Building, and there were around a dozen cops waiting for the Director of Safety to arrive that day. We were gathered in the cafeteria for coffee, and the conversations were mainly about how our different accidents occurred and what would possibly be the outcome.

I had heard the Director of Safety was a cantankerous older man and commented on what I had heard to another cop. There were other people coming and going in the cafeteria that worked in the building, and I never gave a thought to what I had said. We returned to the hallway outside the Safety Office, and were called in one at a time to give our account of the accident. When I stepped into the office, the old man I described in the cafeteria was sitting behind the desk. He was sitting close enough in the cafeteria to hear what I said and needless to say, I was officially reprimanded.

Jesse had been in the district two years before I arrived and already knew quite a few people. Being more familiar, I stood back at times when we came upon a situation with someone he apparently knew.

One 4 p.m. to midnight shift on a warm summer night, around 10 p.m. we received a call of a disturbance and a fight outside a bar in the 1600 block of Margaret Street. Pulling up to the scene, there was around a half-dozen people standing outside the bar. There was a guy lying on the ground with another male standing over him with clenched fists. Before getting out of the vehicle, Jesse alerted me the man standing was a black professional heavyweight prize fighter with a bad temper. As we got out of the police car Jesse asked, "What happened?" The prize fighter turned to Jesse with clenched fists and said, "Nigger, this ain't none of your business, get on outta here."

Infuriated at his remark I said, "I guess you think it's none of my business too."

"I don't know you what the hell you talkin' about white boy."

The prize fighter was well over 6' and all of 220 pounds. With what Jesse said as we pulled up, and the person lying on the ground, I had no idea of the severity of the situation and had my weapon un-holstered holding it behind my leg, something I did quite often as a precaution. Stepping in my direction over the person on the ground, he came at me with clenched fists.

I brought my revolver out at face level at the same time he stepped toward me, and the barrel of my revolver knocked out his front tooth. My action shocked him and he fell backwards over the person lying on the ground. Lying on his back with my gun still at his face I said, "Go ahead, start some shit. I blow your fucking head off and make it look like you did it."

After handling the job Jesse said, "Damn! You even shocked me with your reaction. I don't think you'll have any problems with him from now on."

"Jess, I didn't take this job to get hurt. I'll treat anyone like a gentleman until they try to hurt me." Quoting an old Marine Corps statement I continued, "If they do, I'll try to rip their head off and crap down their neck."

He was right about one thing. From that day forward, it was nothing but respect from him or his crazy brother Curtis. Years later I had to arrest the boxer for murder, but that's a story I'll get into later.

Around a year later, we had to arrest Curtis, the boxer's brother for throwing a lighted bottle of gas into the living room of his mother and father's house. He was apparently pissed off for some reason at his sister, who was asleep on the second floor. To escape the fire she had to jump from the second floor window, breaking both ankles.

On another 4 p.m. to midnight shift around 9 p.m., we received a call to a unit in the housing project of a disturbance. Approaching the unit, we noticed there was a crowd of around 10 people out front talking loudly and pounding at the door. We cleared a path and could hear a lot of yelling from inside. I pounded hard on the front door announcing we were the police, but there was no response, so I tried the doorknob and to my surprise, it opened. There was a man standing in the kitchen doorway with a butcher knife in his hand still screaming at the female in the apartment. I immediately drew my weapon and Jesse grabbed my arm. Wondering why he wasn't preparing for a possible lethal confrontation I asked, "What gives?"

"He isn't going to use it on us, watch."

The guy proceeded to slash at the leather sofa and chair all the while yelling at, who I ascertained by his rant was his wife. The woman just calmly stood there with her arms folded ignoring his verbal abuse until he was finished. After he stopped his triad, he put down the knife and said, "Okay Jess. Do you mind escorting me out?"

I was baffled by the remark until Jesse said, "The crowd outside is her brothers and sister. He's afraid they're going to kick his ass." I laughed as we escorted him to our vehicle and drove him from the scene.

Sometimes domestic disturbances could turn out to be funny. One instance I remember was when we were called to a disturbance and a hospital case. Upon arriving, a man we knew by the name of Jesse Jones was standing in his living room holding a bloody towel on the side of his head. I moved the towel to see how badly he was injured, and observed a pretty sever slash across the ear. We were familiar with Jesse and his wife from being there several times before but it was never this violent.

A couple in their early fifties, the call was always about him coming home drunk most Friday evenings, and his wife complaining about him spending most of his pay at a local bar.

There was a lot of talk between him his wife and another male who was unknown to us.

I said, "Jesse you need to go to the hospital, what happened?"

He replied, "Well Bishop, it's this way. I usually go to the bar right from work, but today I hit the number and figured I'd go home and get my woman and take her with me for a bite. When I came in the house, I heard all this noise upstairs. I creeps up the steps and look in the bedroom," trying to take a swing at the other male with a free hand he continued, "I looks in the bed and I see this motherfucker on top of my woman with a hump in his back like a camel."

"Well how did you get cut?" I asked.

"She cut me!" he exclaimed, pointing to his wife.

After a little more arguing, I convinced him to go to the emergency room to get stitched. As we were walking out the door his wife said, "Don't bring his ass back here. Take him on up to jail and let him out in the mornin.'"

In the police car, he was still feeling pretty good about hitting the number, and quickly forgot the incident at home. It was a relatively quiet night and I asked if he knew any gospel tunes.

He replied, "Hell yeah Randy! I love me some gospel. What you want me to sing?"

Knowing some gospel from being raised in North Philly I asked, "Do you know, Mary don't you weep?"

"Hell yeah! That's one of my favorites."

I began singing using a hand gesture and he immediately picked up on it harmonizing. As he was really getting into it, I handed him the police handset and told him he was on radio. Off and on we sang all the way to the hospital, with my partner shaking his head, laughing the whole way. After getting him stitched, we took him to the district to sleep it off.

Another humorous assignment of a disturbance was at a home in the seventeen hundred block of Meadow Street. Felix Ortiz and his wife were in their early forties, and on occasion were a Friday night calamity. She would go to the corner bar and solicit drinks from a new male patron. Pretending she wasn't married, she would solicit sex and take them home. This particular night, the call was put out as a hospital case.

After arriving we entered the house to find Felix pummeling another male. After calming Felix down the person who was being beaten stated, "He grabbed me in the alley behind the house. I don't know why he's beating the hell out of me. I didn't do anything."

Looking at Felix and his wife for an answer, I asked, "Felix, why did you do it?"

Felix replied with a Spanish accent, "I know he was in here with my wife. I find the circumstantial evidence."

"What do you mean?" I asked.

At the time, some cigarette lighters had clear plastic bases with various objects in them. Some had fishing flies, others had small dice, and the lighter Felix found on the end table next to his bed had a miniature Golf Club in it. After showing it to me he said, "This is the evidence. I don't play golf."

There were more violent confrontations and another I remember, was being called to a disturbance where a Caucasian family lived, who were what we referred to as "dirty-necker's." The Weed family was also a common Friday or Saturday night calamity. The disturbance we went on that particular night had to do with Leo the head of the family.

Entering the house, we saw he was in the process of shooting razor-head arrows into the furniture with a bow. Stepping into the living room, we saw a woman we knew as his wife, trying to come to her senses. She apparently had been knocked cold by Leo, and as Jesse was helping her to her feet, I had a strong premonition Leo was about to point the bow with an arrow in Jesse's direction.

Standing close to him, I punched Leo in the mouth, knocking him over a chair and he dropped the weapon. Would he have used it is an unknown, but intoxicated people could be capable of doing anything, and it's best to err on the side of safety.

CHAPTER 15

Premonitions

Jesse said on more than one occasion, "It's kind of weird working with you, but at times I'm damn glad I am."

My premonitions he was speaking about happened several times and quick action avoided potential harm to both of us.

One incident occurred on a midnight to 8 a.m. shift on a cold February night. Around 3 a.m., we were parked in 1501 wagon on Frankford Avenue facing north toward Pratt Street. We saw a person who appeared to be a young boy coming down from the elevated train platform heading in our direction.

Jesse said, "Hey Randy this kid looks like a curfew."

Rolling down the window he motioned for the kid to come to the wagon. He was a big kid wearing a long heavy coat, and as he stood next to the wagon answering Jesse's questions, I saw shoulder movements and assumed he put his hands in his coat pockets. A premonition hit me that the kid was armed, and as I jumped from the wagon I yelled, "Jesse, watch it! He's got a gun."

Jesse quickly reached out the window grabbing the kid by the coat, and pulled him tight to the wagon. Running around to Jesse's side, I knocked the kid to the ground with one punch. After having him under control we found a .32 caliber revolver in his coat pocket. After taking him to the district for further investigation, we discovered he had just killed his step-mother and grandmother in North Philadelphia. That was the second time in two weeks we had close calls.

The other incident was when we received a call for a disturbance on the second floor in the White Hall Housing Project. The way the building is structured; there are three doors at the entry of a building. One on the left and the other on the right were entrances to first floor apartments, and the middle door accesses the stairs to the second floor apartment. Getting out of the police wagon after we arrived at the location, I noticed the shade go up in a window on the second floor, and the lights go out in the apartment. Walking up to the door, Jesse was in front of me and rang the bell. Having the same premonition, I shoved him to the side knocking him off his feet. Startled, he was about to say something when two shots came through the door. It was a case of a barricaded mentally ill person.

After it was over, Jesse gave me a strange look saying, "You're weird. Sometimes just being in your company makes the hair on the back of my neck stand. How do you know shit like that?"

Shrugging my shoulders, I replied, "Jess, I couldn't give you a clue, but things like that have been happening most of my life."

It wasn't long after that we were working the midnight to 8 a.m. shift in 1501 wagon on a warm mid-August night. There was a flurry of activity until around 2 a.m. then it became relatively quiet. We were parked near Harding Junior High School watching the intersection of Torresdale and Wakeling Streets. Jesse was comfortable in the passenger seat, and I was toying with a loose ring on the flood light handle. It was making a squeaking sound and Jesse, realizing I was in deep thought about something asked, "What's up? Something seems to be bothering you."

After a few moments I replied, "I was just in deep thought about a close relative. He always talks about going to Alaska, and gets a subscription of a Magazine every month called, 'Alaska: The Last Frontier.'"

Shortly after making the statement, we received a radio call to go to the district to transport prisoners to 8th and Race Street where Central Cell is located. It's a place manned by a judge twenty-four hours a day where preliminary arraignments are held.

After returning to the district, we handled a few more assignments then returned to where we were previously parked.

Around 5:30, a call came out at my relative's residence of a hospital case, and the assignment was given to 1503 wagon which covers the Mayfair area. I informed police radio of the relationship and that I was going in on the assignment.

After arriving at the residence, Jesse and I went to the second floor front bedroom. The relative I was referring to about the Alaska magazine was deceased lying on the floor. On the bed was an open copy of a magazine, "Alaska: the Final Frontier."

Apparently, he was reading it when he had the heart attack. Postmortem lividity had already begun, indicating it had been several hours since it happened.

When Jesse saw the magazine open on the bed he brought it to my attention and nervously said, "Randy, I just can't stay in this room with you," then left.

I might add, the time of death was approximately when Jesse and I had the conversation several hours before about the magazine.

Another assignment we responded to was a holdup of a bar at Orthodox and Paul Street. The front door faced the intersection and the rear door faced Paul Street. We happen to be the first to arrive and I said as we exited the police wagon, "Jesse, I'll take the front. You take the side door. Wait till I go in. There has to be a lookout at the side door. He'll run out as soon as I enter, so be careful, he's armed."

As I entered, one of the holdup men was behind the bar, and a second person had the patrons lined up against the wall. The patrons seeing me come in the door hit the floor to avoid the possibility of being caught in a shootout. As other police cars arrived, two officers entered the front to join me, and another stopped where Jesse was standing. Seeing that Jesse already apprehended the lookout, the other officer aided him with the arrest. Frisking him, Jesse recovered a .357 Magnum.

There were many potentially dangerous assignments we participated in, but we were always conscious of each other's safety.

CHAPTER 16

Humorous assignments

On a more humorous assignment, we received a radio call to a residence, "Investigate for an occupant."

That usually meant there was someone who hadn't been seen for several days and most of the time we would find them dead.

This particular call was to a third floor of a three-story property converted into a rooming house. We were met at the front door by the landlady who stated she hadn't seen the occupant since the day before. She further stated they were supposed to meet downstairs to go to church together that morning but she never came down. She also said the occupant, like her, was elderly. When I asked if she had any close relatives, she said she didn't know of any. After getting permission to break open the door, I threw my weight against it and it opened.

It was a two-room apartment with a small bathroom consisting of a stall shower, a small vanity, and toilet. The bathroom, being too small to accommodate a regular door, had instead, a fan-fold-door.

We found the woman as expected, dead in the bathroom. She was a frail woman lying face up, with her arm in a curved position around the base of the toilet. Because the room was too small to get in a collapsible stretcher, we opted to get the reed stretcher from the wagon. Reed stretchers were canvas with wood slats woven in for support, and had straps to bind the person tightly. Their primary use was to get people down sets of stairs too difficult to negotiate with a regular stretcher.

After getting it, I laid it on the floor at the opening of the bathroom, and asked Jesse to straddle the doorway with his feet, standing on the upper corners looking in my direction. That way, I could pull the woman by the ankles onto the stretcher without the fuss of trying to lift the body in such a small area. Getting down on my knees, I grasped the ankles firmly and began pulling her. Her arm came from around the base of the toilet, but with rigamortus, it was stiff and went around Jesse's leg causing him to actually broad jump over me. He came crashing down on the coffee table in the middle of the room, then rolled over on the couch before winding up on his ass on the floor.

Turning to look at him I said, "What the fuck's wrong with you?"

"Randy, I thought the bitch had me," he replied.

I laughed as we carried the woman downstairs and took her to the city morgue.

There were many incidences over the years if Jesse and I could have put on film, would have made television comedy dwarfed by comparison.

Another memorable story was a call to a residence for a demented woman. We were familiar with the house, but that night would top all others. The house was what we called in Philadelphia, a father-son and holy-ghost. These were three-story wooden structures from the mid to late nineteenth century. The ones still existing were at sidewalk level with only a threshold separating the living room from the sidewalk. What hadn't been torn down, were refitted with more modern conveniences like bathrooms and kitchen extensions.

The people who lived there was a man named Russell Renwick and his wife Cleva. She, on occasion, went off the deep end shouting at imaginary things.

It was a blustery November night when we arrived around 9 p.m., the storm-door was closed, but the front door was open. Russell, seeing us at the front door, waved for us to come inside. As I opened the storm door, the cat waiting outside ran in, and the dog inside, took immediate chase barking and screeching at one another running through the house. After we entered, I closed the front door.

Russell, who suffers from emphysema, was leaning against the wall gasping instructions about his wife's current imaginary problem. She was standing in the middle of the living room rocking from side to side shouting, "Cut the lights! Cut the goddamn lights."

There was only one light suspended by a cord from the ceiling in what was considered a dining room, and a set of steps accessing the above floors between that room and the living room.

There was an intoxicated mailman sitting on the steps still in full uniform seemingly unmoved at what was taking place, and when Jesse asked him why he was still out on his route, the mailman opened his bag and began pulling out letters. As he looked at each one, he began reciting a list of liquors, throwing the letters one at a time on the floor, "Tokay, Muscatel, Thunderbird, Gin, Vodka," and so forth. There was a person upstairs who was apparently trying to sleep, and began banging on a radiator hollering, "Knock off all that God damn noise down there!"

Jesse, attempting to speak with Mrs. Renwick, asked if she wanted to go to Friends Hospital but could only get one reply, "Cut the lights! Cut the God damn lights."

In the meantime, the doorbell rang and Jesse went to answer it. We hadn't realized the wind was opening the storm-door causing it to make contact with the bell, and when he didn't see anyone, he returned to speak with Cleva. When he asked again about going to Friends Psychiatric Hospital, her reply was the same, "Cut the lights! Cut the God damn lights."

The dog was still running through the house barking in pursuit of the cat, and Russell was nowhere in sight. In a few minutes I heard a loud noise of dishes falling to the floor and went to the kitchen to investigate, while Jesse was still trying to communicate with Mrs. Renwick. Getting to the kitchen, I observed Russell standing at the sink. Trying to get a drink from the faucet, the pots and pans along with the dirty dishes stacked up on the drain-board fell on his head. He couldn't get free, and was literally drowning standing up. After making sure he was alright, I helped him sit down on a kitchen chair then returned to the living room.

The doorbell had rang again and for the third time Jesse was about to answer it when I told him about the storm-door striking the bell. Opting to listen to what I said, he returned to Cleva still trying to communicate. The person upstairs was still hollering, "Knock off all that God damn noise!"

The mailman was still going down the list of liquor, tossing what was left of the letters from his bag onto the floor. When the bell rang again, with the knowledge of the storm-door causing it, we opted to ignore the problem. In a few moments the front door burst open, and Mrs. Renwicks' crazy sister Flora, came running in. She had a nervous rabbit twitch with her nose when excited, and getting between Jesse and Cleva, she began to shout, "These God damn cops ain't takin' you no where!"

At that point, I was sitting on the arm of the sofa, laughing while observing this human comedy. Jess chuckling said, "Man, you ain't no help! What are we going to do?"

"I'll show you," I replied.

At that point, the storm-door hit the bell again and knocked out the electric power to the house, causing complete darkness throughout the chaos.

After backing the police wagon against the front door, we put Cleva, Flora with the rabbit twitch nose, Russell, the mailman, and the person upstairs along with the dog and cat, and drove to Friends Mental Hospital.

After arriving, I backed the wagon to the front door of the facility and Jesse held the front door open. As soon as I opened the wagon door, the cat jumped out first, heading straight for the open door of the building with the dog in hot pursuit. After herding the occupants into the lobby, we left.

Laughing while shaking his head Jesse asked, "How are we going to classify this job?"

"Minor disturbance adjusted," I replied.

Another incident we were called to of a demented female was in the housing project. Upon arrival, we were met by a woman we had previously encountered who stated her sister was having a problem with an imaginary person. We knew the sister was married to a person whose nickname was Blue. He was shot and killed by the ex-boyfriend by the nickname of Jenks, who was incarcerated for the crime. When I asked what the problem was, the sister stated. "It's this way Bishop. She was married to Blue, and Jenks shot Blue and killed him. Now she sees Blue in her black cat."

I looked at Jesse and he looked at me, realizing the only thing we could do was take her to Friends Mental Hospital. Upon arriving, there was an oriental doctor we previously encountered on duty. After some conversation of why they were brought in, he questioned them.

After hearing the statement from the sister, he looked totally confused responding, "Mister Jenks? Blue in a black cat? I give you a shot; something to make you relax. Okay?"

Her reply was, "You ain't givin' me no mother fuckin' shot."

The doctor replied, "I give you a pill, you come back tomorrow."

Even as compassionate professional people can be, sometimes a situation becomes too intolerable to deal with.

Among many humorous calls over the years we were together, there was another incident I can recall. We were called to a residence where a neighbor of an elderly female stated she hadn't seen the old woman for two days. Again, that probably meant we would find the occupant dead. Upon gaining entry, we searched every room without seeing the resident. There was but one more place to look, and that was the basement. Opening the door, we saw an elderly woman lying at the base of the stairs with grocery items scattered about. Going down the stairs, we were surprised the woman was still alive.

Apparently, she fell attempting to put grocery items on a shelf just inside the basement door. She stated she had been there for two days trying to survive by eating a bag of chocolate chip cookies, and was lying in a puddle of excretion and urine with a host of flies buzzing around.

Retrieving the stretcher from the wagon, I opened it and placed it next to the woman. I bent down to grasp the torso while Jesse grasped the legs to lift her onto the stretcher, and as I began to say something to the effect about lifting the person, a fly went directly in my mouth and down my throat.

"Did I just see a fly go into your mouth?" Jesse asked.

"Yes. And it went all the way down, and went down smooth too. It's probably being attacked by my stomach acid by now."

After placing her on the stretcher, Jesse gagged then ran to the laundry-tub and heaved up the lunch he had just consumed before the radio call. I laughed as we carried the stretcher up the stairs and out to the wagon.

Handling jobs like that didn't bother me and several were pretty gruesome. We had an occasion on a 4 p.m. to midnight shift to get a call to an elevated railroad siding at Bridge Street and Aramingo Avenue, an industrial section of the lower-end. The request was from the lieutenant and car who received the assignment of a dead body discovered along the tracks.

After arriving, we saw the victim's body lying sideways to the tracks with the head completely severed at the neck. There wasn't much blood, but the head of the victim was upright staring in our direction with a grimaced look, something straight out of a Hollywood horror movie. It was a 15-year-old boy who was hopping freight cars for a ride. He apparently lost his footing, and fell beneath the wheels of the boxcar. Wearing a leather jacket, he couldn't pull himself free, and the head was severed at the neck as though it was guillotined.

Jesse and I put the body on the stretcher and I looked at him, the lieutenant and the operator of the police car who had the assignment, to see who was going to pick up the head. After a few minutes I said, "If we wait any longer the head's going to ask one of us to pick it up."

It drew a laugh, and seeing there wasn't going to be a volunteer, I picked up the head by the hair and said while looking at it, "Was it worth losing your head over a little train ride?" then placed it between the legs of the body. As we strapped it down the lieutenant said, "I'm glad you did it. I wasn't about to." Jesse just shook his head as we carried the body from the scene.

Other than the putrid smell of a decaying body, burn victims also have a horrid odor. Most of the time if we could have the medical examiner's office come to a scene, we let them handle it because they carried body bags.

I recall one such assignment where they were involved. The owner of a Victorian home converted into small apartments, called the police to complain about a foul odor coming from one of the units. It was on the third floor and as he guided us up the stairs I asked, "How long has it been since you last saw the tenant?"

"It's been about a week, why?"

"I believe the odor is a decaying human body," I replied.

Stopping at mid-stairs seemingly reluctant to continue he asked,

"Do you think it's that bad?"

"I'm afraid so. That's a smell you'll never forget."

Handing me the key to the apartment he said, "I don't think I want to see it. You have my permission to go in."

We watched as he went past us retreating to the lower floors.

Jess and I continued up the stairs to the apartment and opened the door. Even with Vicks under our nose the smell was putrid. We found the maggot-infested body on the bed and I quickly opened all the windows. We called for the medical examiner's office and awaited their arrival. There was a small portable radio in the living room and I turned it on to pass the time.

After they arrived and moved the body into a sealed body bag to remove it, Jess and I were still in the apartment waiting for a relative who lived close by, to come and collect personal items. It suddenly dawned on us the music we were listening to was fading. Looking over the banister Jess said, "You can bring the radio back."

One of the men from the medical examiner's office had taken it.

Another notable assignment we had, was a call to a Victorian home converted into apartments. After we arrived, we were met by four men who appeared to be in their late twenties to mid-thirties. They were all wearing T shirts, and if a person had to judge the character of the group by their obvious muscular physiques, it could only be one conclusion. They were all body builders.

We asked what the problem was and were told their friend George lived in an apartment on the third floor. The apparent spokesman of the group stated George hadn't been to work for two days, and it was out of his character not to call out sick. He further stated George didn't show up the previous evening at the gym they belonged to for a weight lifting contest, and seemed to be trying to impress Jesse and I with talking about the event. Jesse and I were becoming weary of their conversation, and I asked George's age. The spokesman told me he was forty-two and in great physical shape, expressing how much weight George was able to bench-press.

I asked where they worked, and he told us they worked in a steel plant located at the time on Aramingo Avenue. I then asked whether he lived alone or with a female companion, and he stated George lived alone. When I asked if he had a relative close by he may be visiting, they said they didn't know of any.

Entering the building, I looked at the mail boxes and saw a name of the manager. After ringing the bell, a person stepped into the hallway identifying himself, not only as the manager, but the owner of the building. I asked if he had seen George yesterday or today and he said he hadn't. After explaining what the concern was, he directed us up to the third floor.

The manager tried the door-key he had but it wouldn't fit, and after several attempts without success, he stated George must have changed the locks after moving into the apartment. He told his friends he didn't have the authority to break in, but wasn't opposed to them doing it. At that point, I said we couldn't be responsible for securing it if George wasn't at home, and the spokesman for the group stated they would take full responsibility if that was the case, and that George would understand.

Standing back, Jesse and I let the leader use his shoulder to force the door open. Quickly entering the apartment, the men called George's name and began searching each room. I happened to enter the bedroom and saw George lying on the bed. He was obviously dead, and I called out to the other people, "I found George the iron worker."

As they entered the room they were shocked. George was naked for the exception of a pair of pink women's panties and bra, and what looked like a Blonde Marie Antoinette wig on. He also had a dozen metal washers tied with a string around his scrotum and a plastic bag over his head. Looking at the plastic bag, there seemed to be a clear substance smeared inside. Removing the bag, the substance smelled like a glue of some sort.

After notifying the medical examiner's office, we stood by until they arrived. While we were waiting, the conversation between his friends, were of shock at what he had done. After the body was removed George's friends along with the owner of the apartment began securing the door.

CHAPTER 17

Detectives

At this point I feel it's necessary to give credit to the detectives we dealt with on our arrests and investigations. Detectives like Kenny Curcio, who I mentioned before. He was a young well mannered meticulous dresser, who always took a professional approach to every assignment. Older detectives like Bill Sloss, John Dugan, Joe Tomassetti, Andy Widger, and John Kadellack, and a few more whose names I've forgotten over the years.

The Sergeant of Detectives Roger Heinzenbacker wasn't that instrumental, and I think his attitude was part of the reason. Lieutenant Constanzo of 2 Squad detectives was a great asset on major decisions, but rarely got involved more than just supervision of cases brought in.

Not casting any dispersions or illusions as to what the Sergeant of Detectives was like; I can only judge by an experience. I was solo one 4 p.m. to midnight shift and received a call to a fight and a hospital case at a bar at Torresdale and Margaret Streets.

After entering the bar, I saw a man holding a bloody bar towel over his left eye. He was obviously in excruciating pain and when I removed the towel, I saw his eye was hanging out of the socket with most of it missing.

After asking the bartender who did it and what happened, he replied, "The victim was arguing with another guy he came in with." The bartender further stated that when he turned his back to serve another customer, the guy he came in with broke the bottom off a beer bottle off and plunged the jagged end into the victim's eye.

My primary interest was getting the victim to the hospital as quickly as possible, and I transported him in my vehicle. After we arrived, I went back to the treatment room with the patient to ask several questions. When I asked who did it, he handed me his wallet instructing me to take out a blue business card of a contractor. Showing it to him he identified the name at the bottom as the person who assaulted him. After speaking with the attending physician about the injury, he told me the eye most likely couldn't be saved.

Looking at the identification of the victim, I recognized the name as being associated with a priest at Matter Delarosa Church. The priest was a brother, and the victim's sister was married to an influential and prominent undertaker in the Mayfair Section of the city.

After filling out my report, I took it to Northeast Detectives. Detective Tomasetti took the report and I alerted him about the influential status of the victim. He immediately referred it to the Detective Sergeant who was indulged at the time consuming a hoagie. After Detective Tomasetti filled him in on the assignment, the sergeant slovenly let out with a belch saying, "Arrr! That gives me gas."

I looked at Detective Tomasetti and he looked at me. With a shrug of his shoulders he said, "Don't worry about it Randy, I'll take care of it."

I resumed patrol and that was the last I heard about the job that tour.

We were off the following day and as I mentioned, I had a small concrete contracting business on the side. I was doing a concrete sidewalk on Clark Street in the northeast when a detective's car abruptly pulled up behind my dump truck. I was sitting on the tailgate eating a sandwich when Detective Sergeant Heinzenbacker from 2 Squad, quickly exited the vehicle and hurriedly approached me. He was wearing shorts and a pair of sandals with a tropical leisure type shirt. Seeing his nervous demeanor, I immediately realized the report he neglected last evening had repercussions.

Standing in front of me he nervously asked, "Hey Bishop, what about this job from last night?"

I couldn't resist giving him the same answer he gave me and Detective Tomasetti when we confronted him with it. I don't normally belch, but did everything I could to muster one replying, "Arrr! That gives me gas!"

His face grew red with embarrassment and I think I got my point across about taking care of your job when you're supposed to be doing it.

CHAPTER 18

The Burglary Detail

In the fall of 1975, I was asked to go in plain clothes on the burglary and robbery squad to replace a former Police Academy classmate, who became the new partner with Jesse on 1501 wagon.

The burglary squad assignment was with a cop from another squad by the name of Jimmy Nielson, someone I hadn't previously known. The burglary detail, as we called it, was an assignment with no definite hours. We would check the crime reports coming in, what time of day they occurred and the location, adjusting our hours accordingly. At the time about 80% of the crime was still centered in the lower end of the district, and being familiar with it put us at an advantage. Sometimes we would use an unmarked police vehicle, sometimes our own. Within the first two weeks without radio calls, we made several arrests for burglary of autos, and two purse-snatch arrests. It was something different and I was enjoying the challenge.

According to the crime maps, the lower end of the district was becoming plagued with bar robberies. There had been five within the two-week period occurring between 8 p.m. and 11 p.m., the busiest time for the 4 p.m. to midnight shift.

It was reported the perpetrators were black and in their early twenties. A bar owned by a white person and long time resident one block from the project, and two owned by black people only several blocks from the housing project were never touched. That indicated to me the possibility of the bar owners possibly knowing the people, and that sort of narrowed the search to locals being the perpetrators.

There were several bars that hadn't yet been robbed several blocks north of the project, so we staked ourselves out on a one-way street that had direct access to it. It was fall, and the week we staked ourselves out was cold and rainy.

At the time, we were using my partner's private auto, and around 10 p.m., we were about to change to another location when an auto sped by. As soon as it passed, a call came out of a robbery at a bar several blocks away with the description of that vehicle, and we quickly gave chase. Not realizing we were the police, we sped off to catch up to the speeding car. It pulled up to a residence on Orthodox Street and we were able to get the operator and passengers before they entered a house.

The first several months working the burglary detail we were able to make quite a few arrests for burglaries of businesses along Frankford Avenue. The entry to the businesses was always from the second or third floor rear windows. At one time, the second and third floors were generally occupied by store owners and their families. Through time as the owners moved away, those floors were used strictly for storage.

The buildings weren't designed for security and it didn't take much effort to breach the alarm systems. Even with a silent alarm security system, it still left the front and rear doors secure. The responding police couldn't tell there was a breach of the building, unless they happen to see someone inside, or until the alarm system agency arrived, and by that time, the burglars would have fled over the rooftops.

There seemed to be a rash of burglaries on the east side of the 4500 block, and the stores broken into were a novelty shop, small clothing store, and a sneaker store. By the items taken from the businesses along with the small amounts of cash taken from the register, we realized it must have been kids.

After getting permission from the novelty store owner, we staked ourselves out on the rooftop of the store. Around 10 p.m., I saw a shadow of two people climbing down a drain spout from the third-floor roof. They were able to gain access to the third floor, by walking the elevated train tracks which were at rooftop level. We watched undetected until they broke into the building then placed them under arrest. We were correct in our assumption they were young kids, two brothers ages 14 and 16. The 16-year-old, I had arrested two weeks before for breaking into coin machines at a local car wash.

In the 4100 block of Frankford Avenue was a three-story well known industrial laundry facility. There was a call of a silent alarm one evening at around 10 p.m. and Jimmy and I responded. When we arrived, there was a police K-9 Unit already on the scene. Being in the building before, I was familiar with it. I found an opening in one of the security screens covering the windows and climbed in. After opening the front door allowing the other police to enter, we began to search the building. The second floor is where the main office was located, and the door to the office was locked, but I could see through the glass window the office had been ransacked.

Shining my flashlight in the room, I noticed a ceiling panel missing in the office and saw a loose panel outside the office just above my head. The K-9 Unit was there and the dog was growling looking up at the ceiling. I took a piece of 2"x4" leaning in the corner and pushed up on the loose ceiling-panel, and a man fell out of the ceiling. Before he hit the floor, the dog was on him. The K-9 officer pulled back the animal and we made the arrest. The burglar we arrested was the father of the two teens we arrested for the burglaries on Frankford Avenue, and I made the remark to the other cops, "It must be sort of an 'all in the family situation.'" That brought a laugh from the other cops in the room and we let the security company handle securing the business.

Speaking about security companies, on several occasions I had been at the scene of an open property waiting for them, and upon their arrival, was surprised to see the responder was someone I recognized as having been arrested.

At the time, there was a freight-loading railroad station, at Church and Tacony Street, amidst many manufacturing companies. I worked there part time when I first arrived in the district, and was familiar with it and the surrounding area. There were only a few houses on Church Street, and at the end of the commuter day around 8 p.m., it was generally quiet, and the freight station, as well as the loaded boxcars, became an easy target for burglaries.

Once a boxcar was loaded, it only required a security seal, a metal ban with a federal code number placed through the lock mechanism. Any breach of that band was considered a federal offense, and would automatically bring the F.B.I. into the investigation.

All a person had to do is cut the band, which was easy enough to do, and the booty was there for the taking. Hanger packs of suits and coats from the textile industries still in the city, lighting fixtures from a major lighting company on Erie Avenue, probably the biggest in the world, and carpets from rug mills still in operation.

Knowing the owners, I received permission to stakeout the office, which allowed us to view the entire loading platform and boxcars.

The second night of the stakeout, we watched as a U-Haul trailer backed against the loading platform. One man got out of the driver's seat and opened the rear door of the truck, where two other men exited.

The first stood as the lookout, while the second and third broke the seal of a boxcar and began to unload a few hanger packs of suits. After they had two or three in the truck, we made our move with guns drawn. After placing them under arrest, we had them transported to the Detective Division. The F.B.I. was notified and through their investigation, it was discovered one of the men had a brother working at the freight station. That's how they were able to pinpoint the right boxcar.

There was another arrest late one summer night for a burglary of a boxcar in the Tacony area. Kids had broken into a refrigerated car on a railroad siding. After bringing them to the district, there was some debate as to what to do with the refrigerated items that were now defrosted. I had read in the police directives before, the police department policy was to take the food to orphanages, but my suggestion was hotly debated by the corporal. At the time there was an orphanage on State Road near the Tacony Palmyra Bridge, and after my statement was confirmed by night command, the orphanage was the recipient of the goods.

The 15th District has a unique distinction. They happen to have the only intersection in the country of having a cemetery on all four corners, at Cheltenham and Frankford Avenues. While I was in the 15th, the 1600 block of Granite Street was a hangout for homosexuals, as we referred to them at the time.

That particular block intersected Frankford Avenue, adjacent to the Bridge & Pratt Street train and bus terminal. The Ellis Theatre on the corner had turned into an X-rated movie facing Frankford Avenue, and across the small street was the side of a department store. With the way they were situated, both buildings presented a wall almost the length of the 1600 block, and at the end of the buildings was a parking lot. After the commuter rush in the evening, the street was pretty much unoccupied, for the exception of people hanging out, hoping to score soliciting sex. Once the score was made, a convenient place to perform the sex act was in one of the four cemeteries.

Occasionally, there was a report of a strong-arm robbery, but most times it was only a failure to pay after sex. One night there was a significant beating administered to a person in one of the cemeteries who had been solicited, and within a few days it happened to a different person.

While interviewing that victim in the emergency room to get a description of the assailant, we discovered that, like the first person, his injuries appeared to be for more than just a monetary dispute. He had been struck on the head with a hammer several times and robbed. By the extent of his injuries we realized it would only be a matter of time before the beating was severe enough to cause a death.

After several more incidences over the next few weeks, we began to get closer with the description of the suspected person. I hadn't shaved from the time I went on the burglary detail and had quite a bit of facial hair. I dressed like a longshoreman, and with the permission of the owner of the Theatre, I staked myself both inside and outside of the Theatre, concentrating mainly on the outside.

When a car would come through to pick up someone, I would jot down their license tag to identify the owner of the vehicle. To my surprise, some of the license plates of people soliciting homosexual encounters were married men with children, some from New Jersey, prominent people who drive Mercedes and Cadillacs. I was solicited several times but the person we were looking for drove a late model Dodge.

The second week without a contact, we heard of another possible beating. A person walking their dog through the cemetery discovered a dead body. I was within walking distance and I went to the scene.

Looking at the person on the grave slab, he appeared to be neatly laid out as if he was the person who was buried, and I recognized the face as someone who frequented the 1600 block. He too appeared to have been beaten with a hammer. Other than the body, there was no other evidence at the scene.

For the next several weeks, there were no more beatings, and without success, we ended the detail. Whether it was because the person was scared by the murder they committed, I wasn't sure, and whether they were ever caught is still unknown to me.

While still on the burglary detail, we made several more arrests for strong-arm robbery, and a purse snatch, but to me, the detail was wearing thin. Several weeks later, I voluntarily returned to 2 Squad.

CHAPTER 19

Holiday spirit

The Christmas holiday was coming on and with two small children, I wanted to be home a little more in the evening hours. The other reason and probably closer to the truth, it seemed like every year before the holiday, there was a traumatic event that totally destroyed my Christmas spirit.

Other than crime that comes with the holiday like purse snatches and thefts, there's also a personal experience. The oncoming holiday always produces the highest amount of suicides.

Not long after I came to the district, I received a radio call on a Christmas Eve, Sunday day-work shift to a meet the complainant. At the time the neighborhood was upper middle-class, and going up the front steps, I noticed most of the homes displayed outside Christmas decorations, except the home I was called to. It had no outward sign of the holiday.

After ringing the doorbell, I was admitted to the enclosed porch by a child who appeared to be around six-years-old. The inside of the house like the outside, had no visible sign of the holiday. The enclosed porch was cold, and opening the door to the living room there wasn't much of a temperature difference.

There were two other children younger than the child that admitted me, and after seeing me enter the room; they fled behind a man in a wheelchair who looked to be in his late 30's. The linoleum on the floor was dirty, and had several cereal bowls with remnants of Cheerios scattered about. Several dirty diapers were in the array and the youngest about a year and a half, had a soiled diaper hanging around his knees, probably from the day before. Testimony to that, he had what appeared to be a severe rash on his legs and bottom.

Stuffing on the sofa and chair arms was visible, and there was only a lamp with a broken shade on an end table for light. It didn't take much to realize they were in a state of destitution.

When I asked if the mother of the children was present, the man in the wheelchair said, "My wife couldn't take the situation any longer and walked out several days ago."

There wasn't much I could do other than contact Child Welfare. At the time I was single, but it still had an adverse effect on me, especially when I visited my young nieces and nephews that evening and saw the abundance they were gifted with.

After lunch that same day, I received another radio call to a residence in the 4700 Block of Penn Street. They were Victorian twin homes built around the late 19th Century. After arriving, I was met by a man who stated his friend lived there alone and he hadn't heard from him for two days. When I asked if he could have possibly gone to a relative for the holiday, he said he had no relatives.

The door was locked but I found a side window that wasn't. After climbing into what appeared to be the dining room, I opened the pocket door to the hall. Looking up, I saw a person I presumed was the owner hanging from a banister on the second floor. After admitting the friend, I called for the sergeant and a wagon crew to help remove the body.

* * *

The following year I was working the 8 a.m. to 4 p.m. on Christmas Eve when I received a radio call of a shooting and a hospital case.

After arriving at the residence, I noticed that the front door was open and several children were gathered in the living room crying. A person who seemed to be the mother of the children was hysterical, stating her husband shot himself and was in a second floor bedroom. Hurrying up the stairs, I found him lying on the bed with an obvious gunshot wound to the head. After the body was removed by the police wagon to be taken to the hospital to be pronounced, I questioned the wife. I asked if he had any prior mental problems, or whether she knew of anything that troubled him.

She stated he owned a small convenience store in the Kensington section of the city, and had been robbed several times in the last month. She said he became nervous and distraught over the events and hadn't opened the store for the past week. Although she tried to lift his spirits, he became further depressed and reclusive for not being able to take care of his wife and five children.

As I walked out the front door, the scene of the children crying was enough to ruin anyone's holiday spirit, and I realized the father didn't just take his own life, he ruined Christmas for his family for years to come.

There was another notable incident Jesse and I were called to, only two days before Christmas. The assignment was a hospital case at a catering establishment at Aramingo and Bridge Street. Entering the building, we noticed a person attempting CPR on a young girl lying in the middle of the dance floor. We discovered it was her husband. The event was a Christmas Party for the employees of a nearby business.

The young girl's face was already blue and I felt for a pulse. There was none but we continued with CPR until the Fire Rescue Unit arrived. The husband was frantic and had to be controlled by other people at the event. When Fire Rescue took the girl, the husband went along.

After the body was removed, we posed a few questions about what happened to the other attendees. We learned the girl was 25-years-old, and recently the mother of a child. She was taking some sort of muscle relaxer and had a few drinks just before collapsing.

Another assignment was on the 4.pm. to midnight shift Christmas Eve. Around 11:30 p.m., we received a radio call of a hospital case at a Catholic Church. Entering through the front door, we saw there was a crowd of people around a person lying in the middle isle.

One of the people was performing CPR on a middle-age man, and there seemed to be several people very upset observing what was taking place. The man and his family were attending the 11 p.m. Mass when he was struck down with a heart attack. Jesse and I did what we could do, but to us it was obvious the CPR was in vain. After Fire Rescue arrived, they took him to the emergency room.

Another holiday detail that would try the patience of a saint was the New Year's Parade detail in center city. It was always a ten or twelve-hour day outside with little relief from the cold. Out of the 23 years in the department, I only had the occasion of missing two. One was due to weather conditions that put it on another squad and the other by being injured on duty. The injury was sustained several days before the parade, and it was because I had a cast on my right hand.

I was working solo and went in on a disturbance call with another officer. I was several minutes behind the other officer arriving, and walked up the front steps to the house. It was an older home from around the turn of the century and the front door was open. As I stepped inside I saw the other officer, Bob Rice speaking with someone at the end of a long hallway. There was a pocket door to the living room behind him where a male emerged with a baseball bat in his hand. He didn't realize I was behind him and when he raised the bat to strike Bob, I punched him in the back of his head.

After dropping the bat he fell to the floor. Surprised, Bob quickly turned around. The person I struck was dazed and after Bob handcuffed him, he saw I was holding my right hand in pain. He looked at my hand and before he could say anything, I said, "I already know Bob, it's broken."

After reporting to the district, Bob drove me to Philadelphia General Hospital for treatment. The hand was put in a cast and that was my ticket for the next few weeks off. For a lack of better words for the institution, to this day I can't straighten my little finger on my right hand.

The only time other than that incident I was off duty with an injury happened when I was assigned to a police wagon in the 12th District, in West Philadelphia.

It was a detail I can't quite remember, and my partner Tommy and I reported in. We were assigned to a police wagon and after roll-call we went outside to check the vehicle. The 12th District at 61st. and Woodland is on a commercial strip in the extreme end of West Philadelphia. A firehouse faces 61st in the rear of the police station and the rest of the block is residential. Being a crowded area, parking was at a premium, and the previous wagon crew parked on the sidewalk on 61st street next to the building. My partner was in the driver's seat and I was standing at the curb attempting to safely back him off the sidewalk.

There was a transit bus speeding up 61st, heading for the transit-stop at Woodland Avenue, and I held my hand up to stop the wagon until it passed. Just as it was passing, the wagon slipped off the curb and bumped me towards the side of the passing bus. The access door to the bus engine was loose and as the bus passed, the access door came open and caught the side of my trousers, completely defrocking me. I wasn't injured that badly but it was my ticket for being off from the Friday before Labor Day and the week after. To this day when I speak with Tommy about the incident, we laugh.

CHAPTER 20

Chief Surgeon Detail

In the summer of 1977, Frank Zornek, who had been the driver for the chief surgeon of the city for several years, asked me to fill in for him. He was having a surgical eye procedure that would keep him from performing his job for several months. Apparently, the officer assignment with the chief surgeon had been from the 15th District for years, an assignment where a suit and tie were required. Every morning, it was my job to pick up the chief surgeon at his residence in Mount Airy, and drive him to the Civil Service Building in Center City. It was a day work assignment with weekends off, and as it was summer, I knew it was something I would enjoy.

There was an incident that took place while I was detailed there. Every so often police and fire personnel would get summoned to the chief surgeon's office for a physical checkup. One early summer day, Don Lee was summoned, and I happened to meet him on the elevator heading for his appointment. Don, as I explained before was on the heavy side, probably in the area of 280 pounds.

While getting his examination the attending nurse was having a problem getting his blood pressure. After consulting one of the physicians a doctor looked in on him. The doctor at the time was an older man with poor bedside manners, and that was a moniker given to him by the two other physicians who were in the same office.

After checking Don's signs he said to the attending nurse, "Don't worry about it. By the looks of him he'll die of a heart attack within a year anyway."

I heard what was said and could only imagine what Don was thinking. He happened to be finished his examination at the same time the chief surgeon and the attending doctor were leaving for the day. We got in the same elevator and Don questioned the examining physician about his diagnosis.

He said point blank to Don, "I'm as serious as the heart attack you'll assuredly have." Don asked what he could do to change that diagnosis and the doctor replied, "Go on a diet of tuna fish and peas. Drink plenty of water, and if you have to drink alcohol make it Scotch. It's the only alcoholic beverage that won't put weight on you."

When the elevator reached the ground floor we exited. I looked at Don as he walked away, and wondered what was going through his mind.

On a more humorous note, the chief surgeon and his wife had around eight children. Most were grown and already on their own, but there were two in college and one still a senior in high school at home. The chief surgeon and his wife were on a weekend trip from Friday to Monday morning, so I took advantage of it and took a few days off too.

Sunday around noon, I received a call from one of the sons who was a college student. Knowing I was handy with tools, he nervously asked if I could come to the house and repair a chair that was broken during a party he and his brothers had the previous evening.

Before leaving home, I suspected a little more than a broken chair, so I brought a toolbox with various tools and adhesives.

After I arrived, he appeared to be extremely nervous and took me into the house. Just as I suspected, there was considerably more damage than I was told. Surveying the rooms I asked, "How many people were at the party?"

"I don't know. I only invited a few friends. They must have told other people it was an open house party."

There were several pieces of furniture broken and two small holes in the plastered wall. After helping him and two of his friends restore order, I did what I could to repair the damage, and assured him my lips were sealed to what I saw.

The routine with the chief surgeon was pretty much the same daily. The only time the schedule deviated was when a city employee was hospitalized with serious or life-threatening injuries while working. Most of the time those injuries were to fireman or police, which fortunately, never occurred for the several months I was detailed. It came to an end in November of 1978 and I returned to the district, reuniting with Jesse on 1501 Wagon.

CHAPTER 21

Reuniting

The first 4 p.m. to midnight shift in mid November, Jesse and I were assigned to 1501 wagon. Around 7:30, after the stores were closed, we were parked on Overington Street looking toward the avenue. Don was on the beat that night and Jess asked, "Have you seen Don Lee lately?"

"No, I haven't seen him since he had his examination at the chief surgeon's office in early summer. Why?"

"When you see him, you won't believe how much weight he lost."

It was a blustery night and just after Jess said it, Don happened to walk across Overington Street some thirty yards away. He had probably lost around 80 pounds or more since I last saw him, and as he crossed the street, I noticed his trouser legs were blowing like flags.

Jess said, "There he goes now, bucked up against the wind."

We laughed, but I was grateful he took the doctor's advice. We would at times go trout fishing together on our days off, and he was always good company.

* * *

Several weeks later, we had an assignment one 4 p.m. to midnight shift of a small house fire in the 5400 Block of Large Street. Arriving at the residence, it appeared there was no one at home.

After gaining entry, the fireman extinguished the flames. Searching throughout the house, I noticed there looked like what appeared to be a stash of military weapons: rifles, handguns and a few explosives. From John Galliano's and my experience in the Marine Corps, we realized there was more to this than met the eye. The military explosives we found in the basement, was something we were very familiar with. It's called Composition C-4; a clay like substance which burns with a high degree of heat. In the Corps, we would break off a piece and light it to heat our C-Rations. Although there was no violent reaction to heat, it was electrically sensitive; the slightest electrical charge could set it off. After the sergeant and lieutenant got to the scene, they notified Night Command, who in turn, notified the F.B.I. It was said the explosives later removed by the bomb squad, were enough to destroy several houses on either side of the residence. After the F.B.I. got to the scene, Night Command relieved us and we resumed patrol. Later, we found out the home was the temporary residence of a Government Agent.

* * *

After ten years, like most cops, we began to get job burnout. The district had fallen way below standard with the increased drug use, and crime was pretty much running ramped which added to our frustration. We still mainly relied on informants to make arrests, but were slowly moving away from the aggressiveness we once had. It didn't help with the leniency of the court system, where someone was arrested for a narcotic or other offense and released within several hours. No doubt money or politics played a part in some of that.

When I first arrived in the 15th, there were five new car agencies in the lower end alone. By 1972, they had all left and were either abandoned or converted to other uses. The 4100 block of Frankford had two major auto agencies that were converted to state government offices. One was for Public Welfare and the other for Unemployment.

At the time, there was a union dispute of state employees of some sort going on, and Jesse and I were assigned to stand by in 1501 wagon in case the State Police had a problem with employees manning the picket line.

Viewing the crowd gathered by the front door, there seemed to be several people agitating the employees trying to enter the building to work. There were only four State Police assigned, obviously not enough to handle the job, and when they seemed to be overwhelmed, I called for back-up and we exited the wagon to join them. There was a lot of pushing and shoving with the crowd, and I kept my eye on a person I noticed who seemed to be the most vocal. I assumed he was probably there to agitate, and pointed him out to Jesse as possibly being a union-goon.

He was a big man and began to shove his way toward the state trooper closest to the front of the building. The trooper was trying to hold back the crowd without much success, and when he wasn't looking, the agitator lunged forward, blind-siding the trooper knocking him off his feet. His shirt was torn and his elbows were skinned by the incident.

Jesse and I both noticing, waded through the crowd and I whacked the perpetrator on the head with my night-stick as hard as I could; knocking him to the ground. After handcuffing him, we literally drug him to the police wagon and tossed him inside. Our action seemed to settle the crowd and they moved back. With other police arriving, everything quieted down.

We took the prisoner to the hospital for treatment of his head wound and after being treated, took him to Northeast Detectives for the arrest. One of the cars from the district took the trooper to the hospital for treatment as well, and after he was through, he was transported to Northeast Detectives.

After arriving, there were several people who I assumed to be union representatives, and someone from the state talking with the prisoner. After the conversation they got together with the captain of the Detective Unit. The trooper who was injured was also present, and after some conversation, the trooper stated he wasn't going to press charges on the prisoner.

Protesting, I said, "I don't care what you say, I struck him and opened myself up for a problem. I'm a sight officer and saw what happened. I'm still going to press charges on that creep!"

After signing a paper there would be no repercussions on me, the whole incident was squashed. After the prisoner was released, he walked out with the representatives that were in the discussion.

After they left, I knocked at the divisional inspector's office door. After he stepped into the hallway, I said, "Inspector, if they expect me to stand by and do nothing as a cop gets knocked on his ass, it ain't going to happen." Confused at my remark, I related what just occurred. He walked with us down to the captain's office and after some discussion, the captain pulled the detail. As we were traveling to the lower end, we saw two State Police cars with four troopers in each heading for the Welfare Office.

Slowly but surely, during my time in the 15th, the upscale businesses on the avenue were being replaced by sneaker stores and other low- end businesses. Iron gates that were foreign when I arrived in the district, were now in place over all the store fronts, and the avenue after dark looked like one continuous metal wall from one end of the block to the other. The sectors were readjusted to smaller areas because of the crime increase, and the highest number car in the lower end now numbered ten.

The travesty of the decay of any neighborhood is done to the people left behind. Super markets that move due to theft, only make it more difficult for older people to shop locally, and there was no more obvious case than a woman everyone referred to as "Mom Rose."

Mom Rose was an elderly black woman who lived alone on Tackawanna Street. She believed she was somewhere in her late 80's or early 90's but wasn't really sure. If I can remember correctly, she said she was originally from North or South Carolina, and was the granddaughter of a former slave who came to Frankford in the mid-1800s. From the time Jesse and I worked 158 car we would often stop to see if she needed anything.

I always believed part of policing, was knowing the neighborhood you work in, and the only way that's accomplished is through spending many years there. The "Mom Roses" were a great example.

There was also an old man who kept a garden in the yard of a small factory. Stopping to give him a cold drink when we saw him out weeding on a hot summer day, was small compensation for the community relations it built, and there were many other instances where unsolicited, we would see to an elderly person's personal needs.

As businesses closed, they created a gap for people who worked with their hands. Most people tend not to give into reliance on

Welfare, especially the people who had family responsibilities.

There was a person we knew who lived in the project under those circumstances. Mr. Missouri was raising two young daughters without the benefit of a mother-figure in the home. For whatever reason, his wife became a drug addict, and for the benefit of the kids, they parted.

He worked in a company that was founded in 1865 that manufactured all types of tools, shovels, hammers and axes. He was a laborer and when the plant closed, it left Mr. Missouri literally stranded financially.

Without educational skills, he had to rely on what he knew, and that was working with his hands. He was proficient when it came to auto mechanics, and set up shop in one of the project parking lots operating out of the trunk of his car. We knew his circumstance and sort of looked the other way when we passed through. From time to time, we would stop to chat and it seemed like he was always busy. He not only had project people stopping for repair work, there were people from the neighborhood and even outside the neighborhood bringing their cars for repair. By doing that, he was able to keep a cash flow coming.

One day as we passed through the parking lot, he wasn't there. We assumed he had found a job, but as we were pulling out of the parking lot, he approached us. When we asked why he wasn't repairing cars he told us his car was confiscated by the police outside the city. He said he was doing a tune-up for an employee of one of the businesses who lived in Bucks County. Coming back, he was stopped by the police for lack of a current license plate and inspection sticker, and the car was impounded.

After telling us the circumstances, I asked to use his telephone. I called the police department where the incident took place and identified myself. After giving them a brief synopsis of his circumstance, I sensed the person on the other end of the line was unsympathetic. Apparently they looked in the trunk and discovered the tools he used. Thinking they may have been stolen, they impounded the car to see if there would be a report to that effect. I assured them they were his, and mentioned I would be coming up with him after my shift ended.

Before hanging up the phone the person I was speaking to said, "What you're doing sounds a little beyond the realm of police work." After he hung up I thought, *I wonder if he realizes what police work is really about.* After work, Jess and I picked him up and went to the police station in Bucks County where it took place. After retrieving his tools, we took him back home.

Every Christmas since I entered the 15th, our squad in the lower end always picked out a family we encountered during the year who was in financial straits. After narrowing the search down to one family we would pitch in and buy toys or whatever was necessary to make their holiday a little brighter. That year, we selected Mr. Missouri and his girls to be the recipients. I may add, it became more difficult to select one as the years went by due to the increase in the poverty level in the neighborhood.

The only real disagreement Jesse and I ever had was taking the test for sergeant. John Galliano had already made detective and left, and his partner left the police department. It was my contention the best place to serve John Q Public was right where we were, but Jesse's priority was to be a supervisor.

After our disagreement, I saw the handwriting on the wall, and in 1979, I returned to a patrol car assignment. His partner became a person who formally worked as a Police Athletic League supervisor. The building that was used was formally an old police station at Frankford and Ruan Street that was converted to a gym. The duty was to direct kids in sports or some other endeavor to try and give them an alternative from hanging out on street corners.

Jesse made sergeant and his partner transferred to what we call 5 Squad. That squad was pretty much all fixed assignments from Monday thru Friday, with an occasional detail. Permanent foot-beats were 8 a.m. to 4 p.m., and the 4 p.m. to midnight shift. The squad was also made up of court personnel for district hearings, community relations, and abandon-auto people during the 8 a.m. to 4 p.m. shift.

CHAPTER 22

Routine Patrol

At that point, I was probably the senior member in the lower end, and in a way it was a relief from the pressure Jesse and I put on ourselves. It was routine patrol, and after awhile, I realized that was what I needed. The district was a lot busier but still had its quiet moments. It also gave me the opportunity to arrange squad fishing trips at the New Jersey Shore, and other off duty events like I had years before.

I never lost my initiative to launch a prank now and again, especially when a new sergeant was assigned. One incident was when our squad was working the midnight to 8 a.m. shift. There was a radio-call of an open property at the X-rated movie at Frankford and Granite Streets after closing hours. The new sergeant, on several occasions at roll-call, would remind us of wearing our hats when leaving the vehicle, which was regulation at the time. Several cars answered the assignment including the sergeant. After checking the Theatre, it seemed to be just an open property and we left through the side door. Noticing the sergeant wasn't wearing his hat, before leaving the building I grabbed an inflated sex-doll at the concessions counter and put it in the driver's seat of his police car with his cap on it. Coming out of the Theatre, he looked at the doll shook his head and laughed.

After breaking him in as our supervisor, he became one of the best. He left after a short time when he made lieutenant, and before his police career was over he attained the rank of inspector.

There were other occasions when given the opportunity, I would rattle someone's cage, but it was all in jest, and no one ever became offended.

Another incident that was pretty funny was when I put a white mouse in the briefcase of another cop. Jack was also an ex-Marine who was pretty big. He worked with another officer on 1500 wagon, and on occasion would act in jest like a "Macho Man." Seeing their wagon parked on the ramp of the hospital emergency room, I slipped the mouse in his briefcase. I stood in the doorway of a house adjacent to the ramp and watched as he got in the wagon. Within a few minutes, he jumped from the wagon and threw his briefcase to the ground. Realizing it was probably me who did it he just laughed and picked up his belongings.

Another incident I remember was when I got even with a cop who was recently assigned to the district. He had several years in the police department and for some reason that I can't remember, did me an injustice. Seeing his car parked on the ramp of the emergency room, I went in and retrieved a large irrigation syringe. After filling it with talcum powder, I blew it into the vents in his police car and turned the switch to the air conditioner vents on high.

After getting in his vehicle, he turned the ignition and the powder burst from the vents covering him. I was watching from a doorway across the street and when he jumped from the vehicle, he looked like a snowman. I think he realized it was me who did it, but never confronted me.

On routine patrol I made several notable arrests, but they were largely a result of a radio call. Occasionally, they were the result of pulling over a vehicle for some infraction or another, and finding out the person was wanted.

I was still receiving information from long-time residents about what was happening in the lower-end, but turned whatever information I received over to the younger cops. Occasionally, they would ask me about a particular person or persons, and if possible, I'd give them the information I knew. It seemed as though I was now the Frank Zornek of the lower end.

Being a mentor was not only self satisfying, it was refreshing to know there were still cops looking to do the same job Jesse, John Galliano, and I had done, people who were really interested in doing the job they signed on to do.

One quiet Sunday morning on day-work, I was solo on 159 car and received a radio call to a converted Victorian home in the 4900 block of Penn Street to meet a complainant.

After arriving, I went into the vestibule. The mailboxes indicated there were six apartments in the three-story home, two on each floor, and the call supposedly came from a person living in a third floor-front apartment. The stairway to the upper floors was something unusual. The steps were much higher than the normal seven-inch riser and the tread was much shorter than ten or twelve inches deep.

To negotiate the stairs, a person had to be careful and watch their footing, even while holding onto the handrail. The staircase was around four-feet wide and around fourteen steps high, walled on both sides. Before climbing the stairs, I first looked up and noticed the top of the stairs entered what looked like a blank hallway going to the left and right.

Holding my nightstick in my free hand, I climbed the stairs while holding onto the rail. As I reached the second step from the top, a hand with a revolver came around the corner from my right and pulled the trigger. Quickly reacting, I struck at the hand with my nightstick and lost my balance falling backwards down the stairs. Whoever it was, threw two shots in my direction as I was tumbling down, and to this day, given the small area at the bottom of the stairs, I don't know how I wasn't hit.

There happened to be a member of the squad named Joe Tancredi, coming in on the assignment, just to get the particulars on a squad fishing trip I had scheduled the next day. Entering the vestibule, he saw what had taken place, and after getting to my feet, we heard what sounded like someone throwing their weight against an apartment door on the second floor to the right. I told Joe to call for backups then go around to the rear of the building while I take the stairs.

After he exited the building, I slowly crept up the stairs. Reaching the top step, I peered from floor-level around the corner towards where we heard the door being broken in. There was no one in the hall and the apartment door was ajar. Slowly going down the hall flat against the wall, I pushed open the apartment door. The place was empty and I noticed a rear window open. I heard several shots in the rear of the property and guessed it was gunfire between Joe and whoever shot at me. Looking out the window, I saw the perpetrator. He had climbed the backyard fence and was making his way through the rear yard of the property on the next street. I yelled down to Joe where he went, and by the time I reached the yard, there had probably been a second assist officer call put out by neighbors and police cars were streaming in from different sectors, along with a stakeout unit.

The perpetrator, realizing he couldn't get away, took a woman hostage on Leiper Street on her way to church. He had a tight grip around her neck, but by that time he was completely surrounded by police. After what seemed like a ten minute stand-off, he loosened his grip and the woman was able to pull loose falling to the ground. As soon as she did, shots came from me and the stakeout unit. Approaching him, I noticed that the guy was obviously dead, and I kicked the gun away from his hand.

After the shooting, a person approached me identifying himself as the person who lives on the third-floor of the apartment building, and stated he was the person who called the police. Enraged that the call came out as a routine meet the complainant, I asked who the deceased was. He told me they were cellmates in prison, and the deceased was currently out on parole with fourteen years back-time. He further stated he was out to kill him, and when I asked why, he didn't give me an answer.

I shoved him around a little yelling, "Why the fuck didn't you tell the police dispatcher what he was going to do?"

Shocked at my reaction he said, "I did tell the person who answered the phone. I told him the guy was probably carrying a gun and out to kill me too!"

After homicide unit and crime lab arrived, I took the .357 Magnum to ballistics. I had to go to homicide to fill out paperwork but before I did, I visited the police radio-room. After entering, I went to the console that broadcasts our district where a civilian and a policeman are assigned.

Infuriated, I asked who answered the call, and when the civilian said it was he who answered it, I snatched him from his chair. I was about to pummel him when the lieutenant from the radio-room grabbed my arm. He assured me there would be a retribution for his action, and reluctantly, I left it at that. After the interview at homicide, I returned to the district.

Later, I discovered a bullet remaining in the revolver was struck, but for some reason didn't fire. I couldn't recall how many shots were fired by the deceased, but I can only imagine that was the bullet that was struck when I breached the top of the stairs.

One of the things entering my mind after the incident was what Iron Mike said years ago as we parted. *"Be careful. Although you're going to a quieter district, it only takes one asshole to take your life."*

CHAPTER 23

Time for a change

I entered the district on a Friday 4 p.m. to midnight shift and was told I would be the turnkey, the person responsible for the cell-room, instead of working my normal police vehicle. I never held that position and wondered why I was gifted for the assignment. Going into the cell room I realized why, the place was like a zoo, almost every cell was occupied and the noise from the occupants was deafening. I wasn't sure whether it was a punishment for some unknown reason, or whether it was a chance to get rid of me by losing a prisoner.

Several hours into the shift, the captain's clerk entered the cell-room and asked whether I wanted a permanent beat in the lower end on day work. At first I thought he was breaking balls because of the chaos in the cell room, and I was having a rough time with prisoners. I knew a friend of mine had that 5 Squad assignment, but the captain's clerk assured me it was legitimate, and the friend I was referring too was taken off the assignment for disciplinary reasons.

I realized it was probably offered because I was familiar with the neighborhood, and knew quite a few merchants as well as the inhabitants.

I jumped at the opportunity, and leaving the district at the end of the tour, I was looking forward to Monday morning and the new assignment.

The foot-beat was four blocks long on Frankford Avenue without a restriction on either end. It was from Monday thru Friday with weekends off save an occasional detail, something I knew I would relish. It had a major transportation hub at Margaret Street Station with considerable foot traffic and other responsibilities, but I knew I would be comfortable with steady hours after so many years. They say an irregular routine will take ten years off your life span, and I totally agree with that analogy. Days with little or no sleep for one reason or another, or working a different shift for six days has to eventually cost you in the long run.

After working the midnight shift then going directly to center city for a court appearance in the morning without the benefit of several hours sleep wasn't easy. Add the responsibility of children during the day at home, only exacerbates what I called the "rundown syndrome." The whole schedule of changing every six days never lets the body get used to a routine.

Entering the district the first day of the new assignment seemed a little odd. Normally I, like the other members of the squad, would go directly to the roll-room and converse with one another until the sergeant arrived. Today I checked out a hand-held radio and just told the Corporal I was present. Going outside to my private vehicle to drive to the foot-beat I was assigned, I glanced at the day-work squad checking their vehicles, and was glad all that was finally behind me.

The beat was more or less daily routine aside from a few radio calls. After arriving at the beat, I parked in a bank parking-lot at Unity Street. It was an old building circa 1905, when banks were built like gigantic vaults. It had a high wrought-iron fence surrounding it so I felt comfortable leaving it there. After exiting my pickup -truck, I pulled the collar of my coat up a little to protect my neck from the cold winter breeze.

Leather Coats with Sam-Browne Belts worn at the time might have looked impressive, but weren't all that warm, especially on a day like today. It began to flurry, and with the strong wind hitting my face, it felt like I was being hit with a hand full of razor blades as soon as I walked out on the avenue. Even as uncomfortable as it was that day, I wasn't about to complain, I had worse details.

For the first two weeks, I felt it was necessary to acquaint myself with store owners I hadn't previously knew. I made it known I was there for any problems they might have, and encouraged them not to hold back no matter how trivial they thought it may be. I took an interest in looking around their business establishments and pointed to weak security spots and how to reinforce them. I felt that by doing this, they actually realized I was there to help and not someone who just wanted to write parking tickets.

The people who lived in the area that I've known for years, would sometimes stop and tell me how they missed the secure feeling when the Jess and I worked together, and I'm sure they passed on a few positive comments to the different store owners.

Seeing most of them weekly, somehow I felt like I never left working the sector car. At times, they would tell me things that went on in the hopes I would personally try to do something about it, but couldn't do more than pass the information on to whatever squad was working at the time, and had no way to tell if it was being followed up.

On a Monday as I was walking out on the beat, a nice looking well-dressed woman who looked to be in her mid twenties approached me and asked, "Officer, is this a very safe neighborhood?"

"That's a strange statement. What do you mean by that?" I asked.

"I have a friend who's 7 months pregnant. We were supposed to have a baby shower for Bernice on Sunday, but she never showed up."

"Where does she live, here in the neighborhood?"

"No, she lives in Upper Dublin Township in Bucks County."

"Well why are you looking for her down here? Were you originally from this neighborhood?"

"No. We're originally from the Ogontz section of the city, but we moved out to a small town called Glenside five years ago. After she got married, her and her husband bought a home in Upper Dublin."

"How do you know she was here?" I asked.

"My friend gave her a gift certificate for an expensive baby carriage from a store here in Frankford. The store is called Goldberg's. They're supposed to be the best in the city for that sort of thing. Do you by chance know where it is?"

"Yes, I do know the store; it's in the next block. Are you by chance trying to tell me your friend's a missing person? Maybe she hadn't picked it up yet."

"I spoke to her on Thursday. She said she was picking it up the next day, and asked if I could go with her. I was busy making plans for the shower, and told her I couldn't. I asked if she could postpone it until Saturday. She said she couldn't, and told me she was going by herself. I was supposed to take her out to lunch on Sunday so we could surprise her with the baby shower when we got back that afternoon."

"Well, Goldberg's in the next block, let's go and ask if he remembers seeing her, what's your name?"

"My name's Cheryl. What's yours?" she said as she held out her hand to shake mine.

"My name's Randy, Randy Bishop."

Walking into the store Mr. Goldberg said, "Randy, what's new and interesting on the beat today?" as he turned on the lights in the show cases, and display counter.

"Mister Goldberg, this young lady wants to ask you a question."

"What is it, young lady?"

After describing her friend, and the circumstances of why she was asking, he thought for a moment and replied. "Yes, I remember her. She had a gift certificate to pay for the coach. My son-in-law Allen carried it out to her car and put it in the trunk."

"Do you by chance remember what time that was, or have a receipt Mr. Goldberg?" I asked.

"Let me see," he replied as he thumbed through a stack of receipts. He looked bewildered for a moment wondering why it wasn't there, and then suddenly remembered, "Wait a minute. While she was here, she bought a few other things and paid for them with a credit card."

"If she did, the copy would have the time of purchase. Can I see it?" I asked.

"Sure, here it is. It was 3:45 p.m."

Looking at Cheryl, I said, "Well she was definitely here. That was almost three days ago. Does she have any other children?"

"No, this is her first, and she was really excited about it too."

I remember seeing a worried look come over her face. She said, "It's not like Bernice. We've been friends since elementary school. I don't like this at all."

I reminded her that she said she gave Bernice a gift certificate too, and asked what it was for.

She replied, "It's for a baby store in the mall at Cheltenham and Ogontz Avenue, in Cheltenham Township, just over the city line."

I asked, "Did Bernice mention going to that baby store when she spoke to you?"

"I don't remember if she said she was going there too."

With Mister Goldberg listening intently, I told her I couldn't pursue it any further; that mall was beyond the city limits. I asked her if she contacted Bernice's husband about her whereabouts, but she said when she called he didn't seem that concerned. She further stated he mentioned Bernice hadn't been home since Friday afternoon.

"Why didn't he report her missing?"

"I don't know. She told me several months ago they weren't getting along so well. She suspected he was having an affair with his hygienist."

"That means he's a dentist. Did she mention about any arguments they might have had?" At that point I felt a little uneasy to just end the conversation and asked, "Do you have a receipt of the gift certificate you gave her? It probably has a phone number of the store. I'll call and ask if she was there."

Searching her handbag, she pulled out the receipt, "Here it is."

I asked, "Mr. Goldberg could I use the phone?"

"Certainly, Randy. Come around to this side of the counter."

After dialing the number, a woman answered the phone. I mentioned who I was and why I was calling. I then asked if she had the receipts for gift certificates from Friday. After giving her the number, she took a few minutes then replied, "Yes she was here and used the certificate at 5:30 p.m. I remember her. She seemed to be in a rush too. Is there something wrong?" I avoided answering, and instead asked if she could hold a copy of the receipt in case there's a continued investigation.

When I said it, I noticed Cheryl nervously wringing her hands. She asked, "Do you suspect something's happened to Bernice?"

"No, but it's worthy of looking into. I heard you mention living in Glenside. Have you always lived there?"

"No, we we're originally from the Ogontz section of the city. We lived on a small street west of 75th and Ogontz, Windam Street to be precise. All of our friends grew up in that neighborhood."

"At one time that neighborhood was predominantly Jewish. I used to live in that neighborhood too," Mister Golberg added.

I asked Cheryl, "Do you know what kind of car she drives?"

"Yes. It's a four-door silver color Buick LaSabre. She has a Temple University sticker on the back window."

After she said it, I asked Mister Goldberg if I could use his phone again. I called the 35th District where Cheryl said they grew up, while she stood impatiently waiting to listen to my conversation. The corporal answered the phone and I explained the situation. I asked if Lieutenant Miller was on duty and the corporal said he was in the operations room at that moment. I knew the lieutenant from other police details and explained the situation. I gave him a description of the car and asked if the sector car that covers the area Cheryl grew up in, to keep an eye out for it. He agreed, and after a few words about the department, I hung up.

"Will they try to find the car?" she asked.

"Yes. The lieutenant's aware of the situation and he's pretty thorough. We've known each other for years."

I wanted to make another phone call but didn't want Cheryl to know who that phone call was going to, so I escorted her to her car. After reassuring her I would do all I could do to help solve the mystery, she reluctantly drove away.

I went back to Goldberg's and asked if I could use the phone once more. After getting permission, I put in a phone call to the Homicide Unit. I asked to speak with the captain who I knew from the time he spent in the 15th when I first arrived. After Jerry answered the phone, we had a brief conversation about some of the people we worked with in the 15th then I told him the reason for the call. He sounded positive about my assumption the car may be in that area since it was so close to the Cheltenham Mall, the last place Bernice shopped.

I remember thinking about how that day began, and it was in the back of my mind until I reported off. I contemplated driving through the neighborhood myself, but for some reason let it pass.

Later that evening, I received a phone call at home asking me to return to the district. After I arrived, the corporal told me homicide unit wanted to speak with me. After telephoning, the person who answered the phone connected me with the captain. After answering the phone Jerry said, "Randy, you were right. They found the car in the neighborhood you said it would be. The woman was found in the trunk of the car, she'd been brutally stabbed to death.

I received a court notice and had to appear in Montgomery County Court. Although the body was discovered in the city, the homicide took place in the parking lot of the mall that's outside the city. The investigation turned out to be a contract killing solicited by the husband, and was done by a junkie from that neighborhood.

That was one of many cases where the coordinated units within the police department functioned exceptionally well.

As time went on, the beat became routine, and wondered whether I would soon tire from the boredom.

Occasionally, I would walk a few blocks off the beat to check the laundry facility at the project. I knew from working the area, it was a hangout for kids cutting school from Frankford High or Harding Junior High, only several blocks away. If I discovered them there, I would clear them from the facility with a nudge on the backside with my nightstick. If I knew their parents, I would walk them home.

The funny thing about working the same area for so long; is the fact you actually see kids as they grow up. From turning on the sprinkler at the fire hydrant in their neighborhood on a hot summer day as 5 and 10 year olds, those same kids are now in their teens attending the local high school.

With my assignment, I was not only able to continue doing concrete work when spring came, but leading up to that time, I was able to secure work from multiple store owners as well as a local savings and loan bank, and a medical center.

The savings and loan on my beat inherited a group of houses in a takeover of another institution in different levels of disrepair in different areas of the city. It became my job to evaluate the properties and do whatever was necessary to make them habitable for resale.

Through my father's great genes, I had a wide knowledge of how to use tools, and with the help of some of the neighborhood kids after school, I was able to repair some of the one's that were salvageable. I tried to teach them some of what I knew in that respect, but the real purpose and the most important, was to let them know what it felt like to earn, and the good feeling of self-accomplishment. All of them came from broken homes without a father or mother figure present, and I enjoyed stepping into that roll.

Occasionally, I had to thump one of them for getting out of line but there was never animosity between us, and I feel they realized it was for their own good. I happened to have a small surgery at Frankford Hospital that required a few days recuperation. During my stay at the hospital all the kids who worked with me visited.

A few went astray and it was always disheartening to see them give up. This was mainly due to seeing other kids their age with money in their pockets, new sneakers and hadn't gotten dirty accomplishing it. I could never compete with that by paying $5 dollars an hour.

One day, the bank parking lot where I usually park was being repaved, so I had to park my pickup truck on a small side street at Frankford and Kinsey Street, just off the avenue. During the later part of the tour, there was a call of a fight on the highway in that block and I quickly responded. As I entered the street, there were several young kids I knew beating up on someone. When I asked what they were doing, one of the youths who worked with me repairing houses said, "He broke the vent window and was inside your pickup."

The person in question was a junkie in his early twenties who came from another part of the city. I let him go with a warning, and the local kids escorted him to the El Station at Margaret Street. After giving him a warning not to return, they waited until he got on the train.

One day as I was returning to the beat from the project, the sector car working that area saw me off my beat and pulled to the curb. He asked if there was something he could help me with and I assured him I was fine. In the few words of conversation we had, he said something that shocked me.

He said, "I never patrol the project, and don't go there on any disturbance calls unless I have a backup," pausing for a moment he continued, "and I always wait until I think the backup is there first."

As he pulled away from the curb, I watched as he continued down the street. Continuing to the beat I thought, *"If that's what's replacing Jess and I, heaven help the neighborhood."*

That person eventually went up the ladder of promotions and became a police inspector.

I had a humorous encounter with a rookie one day that was notable. I had noticed for awhile by listening to his response to assignments on police radio, he was coming on as a conscientious officer trying to do the job.

There was a report of a strong-arm robbery one day just off the avenue, and he was quick to respond. When I got to the scene, the rookie was just pulling up to the assignment. A witness gave us a description and told us the suspect had gone up the stairs to the elevated train platform. We went up the stairs and noticed a man in his twenties seemingly waiting for the train. His description wasn't exactly as described by the witness, but he was the only person on the platform, and when he saw us, he became nervous. As we approached the suspect, I sort of stood back to see how the rookie was going to handle the job.

The suspect was acting extremely nervous which indicated to us he didn't want to be tested. The rookie asked him a few questions and when he asked him his name the suspect replied, *"Nosmo King."* I waited to see the reaction from the rookie, but he wrote the name of the suspect on his incident report just as he stated.

I chuckled to myself and the rookie asked what I thought was so humorous. I told him to turn around and read the sign on the wall. He looked at it still seemingly confused not understanding why I made that statement.

I said, "Read the first two letters on the sign and put the rest of the letters together." He looked at it for a few seconds then realized my point. The suspect was giving him the name Nosmo King from reading the "No Smoking" sign. The rookie shoved the suspect against the wall and frisked him for identification. After giving radio the suspects name and age, they responded that he was wanted for a bench warrant for failing to appear for a hearing at Common Pleas Court.

After placing the suspect in a police wagon, he turned and made a funny statement. He said, "I guess you think I'm pretty stupid?"

I replied, "No, there are many tricks to the trade. You'll learn that as time goes by but you're off to a good start."

The police department always had female police officers, but they were more or less relegated to Sex Crimes Unit or Juvenile Aid, any situation where a woman would be needed.

I remember working the midnight to 8 a.m. shift on 159 car when the first female officer was assigned the lower end. Before hitting the street the sergeant said, "If she gets a call to the project, go in on the assignment with her."

Looking at him I replied, "Do I get part of her pay?"

"No. Just do it. That's what they want downtown."

I shook my head as I walked out to my patrol car.

Most women police officers I saw; didn't have the physical strength to handle the job, but like anything else, there were exceptions. One in particular was a tall, dark-skin black female named Renee. I had the occasion to get a call to the elevated train stop at the Margaret Street Station of a fight on the platform. Walking upstairs to the platform, one of the people coming down told me there was a female police officer in a tussle with a man. Hurrying up the steps, I saw Renee pummeling the hell out of a guy close to her size. After I helped handcuff the man, she stated he was the person her court case was about, but didn't show up for the case. She was just returning to the district when she saw him on the platform, and when she confronted him, he kicked her.

I had another incident involving a police woman that better reinforces my point. I was at the corner of Frankford and Margaret when a woman approached and said a male had just snatched her handbag. She pointed to a vacant property just off the avenue that was formerly a bar. There was an alleyway leading to the rear of the property and I knew at times it was a hangout for "wineos." As I approached the alley, there was a man and a woman at the end of the building. The property had been boarded up but somehow the rear doorway was open.

I approached the man and woman but unbeknownst to me, there was a second male just inside the rear door who stepped out. As soon as he saw me, he came at me with clenched fists. Sidestepping his movement, I struck him on the head with my nightstick. The female assaulted me and the second male joined in.

They were doing major renovations to the Frankford Elevated Train Stations at the time, and happened to be working on the Margaret Street Station. Someone must have called an assist officer, as I heard the call come out on my police radio. One of the workers on the elevated platform must have seen what was happening, and a few came down the stairs to assist. Before they could get to where I was, a police car pulled up and the female officer looked in my direction then pulled away.

After other police cars and a wagon arrived the situation was under control. Exiting the alley one of the construction workers made the remark, "I don't believe what I saw. When that first car arrived then pulled away, I was shocked."

I agreed with him, but didn't comment. I knew the department was changing, but there wasn't anything I could do about it. The arrest was made, and the purse was recovered inside the vacant building.

At one point there were several changes of command with captains and inspectors over a short period of time, and although I wasn't really sure, I think it had something to do with video poker machines in bars.

The inspector of the division at the time was promoted to chief inspector, and shortly thereafter in a federal investigation, he was put on trial for extortion and found guilty. As a result, he was suspended from the department and served some jail time. A few other lower commanders quickly retired, and I suspected it was to avoid the same fate.

The hypocrisy of the man, was coming down to my beat questioning me about a black person who owned several local bars. I didn't realize it at the time, but that's one of the people who made the formal complaint to the F.B.I. about the extortion.

Jesse and I pretty much lost contact with one another save an occasional phone call for several months, but when he did call, I thought it was only to more or less reminisce. Being a partner with someone for so long, you really get to know the person's character. You actually spend more time with them than a wife or any other relationship, and when something's amiss you can sense it. At the end of the conversation I felt he wanted to desperately add a comment, but for some reason was hesitant.

One day after reporting off duty, I was coming out of the district and saw him leaning against my pickup. After an embrace and a hearty greeting, he asked if we could go somewhere and have a drink. I knew it was out of character for Jess to drink, and in fact, I only saw him take a drink once or twice the whole time we worked together. I realized the seemingly unfinished conversations we had on the phone was probably what was plaguing him, and we went to a bar not far from the district.

Anxious to hear what he had to say, I was surprised when he began to vent his anger. He started by saying he was on the verge of punching out the lieutenant of his squad, and was getting close to doing it.

After calming him down by telling him he would probably forfeit his sergeant stripes, I asked what the problem was. There had never been an incident of racial disharmony with me or Jesse, or in fact, anyone else I've ever encountered. The high school I attended was predominantly black, the neighborhood where I lived was predominantly black, or in the police department up to that point I never encountered it. What he told me gave rise in the belief I may have been wrong. To quote, he said his lieutenant, who was black told him, "Whenever you see a white cop in your squad doing something wrong no matter how minor, I want you to take disciplinary action against them. No excuses, no leniency."

Knowing the Jess' character, that sort of thing had to be what was plaguing him for a long time. My advice was, to try bearing up to it without putting himself in jeopardy, and I believe our conversation was more or less like opening up a valve to release the pressure. I've seen Jesse get angry and although his temper was controlled, everyone has a pressure point. Before we parted at the district he gave me an embrace and made a statement I'll forever remember.

He said, "We been partners through thick and thin. I'll never forget the times we went through together, take care brother."

As he walked away, I wondered whether he would take my advice. Luckily, his lieutenant wound up getting transferred for one reason or another, and Jesse went further up the ladder with a promotion to lieutenant and a different assignment.

CHAPTER 24

Mean Gene

The captain who took over the 15th district was a previous Lieutenant in the Foot Traffic Division. His nickname for some reason was "Mean Gene," but in all the time I knew him he never demonstrated a mean streak. He would raise hell with a situation to get it right, but 5 minutes after the ass chewing it was like it never happened. He was a newly-promoted captain and the 15th was his first command.

He seemed to be conscientious from the first day, and let 5 Squad members as well as everyone else in the district know he demanded no less than the same from them.

He had a cliché of saying "*Big Boy!*" whenever he was about to admonish you for some reason or another, and that phrase became a joke between 5 Squad members when we addressed each other, often using that term. To this day, we still say it jokingly when 5 Squad members get together.

He was meticulous about his personal appearance as well as the district building, but didn't realize the power of City Unions, even over police department demands. There was a new set of interior doors for the entrance of the building that had been stored in the cell-room for at least nine months that I knew of.

After many calls to the maintenance department without success, he asked if I could install them. I took on the job with a helper and was about half way through when a union representative entered the building. He asked where the captain's office was and I pointed to the door. A short time later, I heard loud voices from his office, and shortly thereafter the union representative stormed out of the building.

An hour later, as the captain was watching me put the finishing touches on the door's, his clerk came out in the hallway and told him the police commissioner was on the phone. After their conversation, the captain came out in the hallway and watched as I finished the doors. As he walked back to his office, I heard him quietly say *"I have to work here. Fuck the union ....and fuck the Police Commissioner too."*

Sometimes he would take a drive through the district. If he saw me on the beat he would stop to talk, or pick me up and have me accompany him wherever he was going.

There was an auto body shop in the 4400 block of Paul Street that was a constant complaint of the neighbors. The complaint was the shop parking cars being worked on all over the sidewalk, forcing people to walk in the street. That's where he was heading that morning so he picked me up to accompany him. After we arrived, there were several cars parked on the sidewalk and he instructed me to issue parking tickets. While writing them the owner came out of the building. He began to give me hell for writing them, and I directed him to speak with the captain. As I was writing, I heard the owner confront the captain with a loud voice. I knew Gene's temperament and heard him getting louder, angrily saying, "If I have to detail a man here all day to write tickets for you parking on the sidewalk, that's what I'll do."

I realized he was getting close to a physical arrest, but fortunately, the garage owner realizing it, went back into the building. After returning to his car, it took him a few minutes to calm down before he drove away. He said, "It's only a block off your beat, but try to check on him several times a day."

Reassuring him that I would, we drove away.

* * *

Around two weeks later, he stopped on my beat to speak with me about attending a community meeting, and while we were talking, there was a radio report of a purse snatch around Frankford High School which was only several blocks away.

After arriving at the scene and getting a description of the purse snatcher, it sounded like it might have been a young kid. I instructed the captain to let me out of the car at one end of an alleyway near where the purse snatch occurred, only a block from the high school. I was familiar with the area and knew the alleyway was a direct route back to the school, if in fact the assailant was a student.

After exiting the car, I told the captain to go around the block and stop at the other end of the alley. Just as I figured, the kid was in a backyard, rifling through the pocket-book. Coming out of the backyard, he saw the captain at the end of the block, and turned to run in my direction. I grabbed him by the back of the jacket and ran him down the alley, shoving him head long into the captain's car. He was dazed and after picking him up, I put the handcuffs on.

The captain's car was a newly-issued model he received only the day before, and he noticed a dent where the kids head and body made contact. While rubbing his hand over the dent he yelled, "Hey Big Boy! Look at that damn dent! Why didn't you shove him into a tree or something else?" I was at a loss for words, but making the arrest took precedent over the damage.

Before reporting off that day, I went to the auto body shop on Paul Street and got a business card. When I reported off at the district, the captain's car was still parked in his assigned spot. I knew he was about to leave the building, so I put the business card under his windshield wiper. I stood at the end of the building and peered around to watch as he left the district. After getting in his car, he noticed the card under his windshield wiper and got out again to see what it was. After looking at it, he laughed then looked around to see if I was in sight. Shaking his head, he smiled as he got in the car and drove away.

There was another notable instance I put together with the help of the squad. For Gene's fiftieth birthday, 5 Squad arranged a late afternoon bash at a local Italian restaurant. It was normally closed on Monday, but knowing the owner personally, he obliged us. I knew a few girl strippers from the area and solicited one to do a routine for the occasion. I got together a police uniform complete with, badge, cap and a ticket-book, and instructed her to enter the restaurant shortly after the event began.

The captain's driver delivered him to the restaurant at the appointed time, and was instructed to park close to the corner. During the luncheon, the stripper walked in with a ticket-book in hand loudly demanding, "Whose car is that, parked too close to the corner?"

I was sitting next to Gene and he leaned towards me quietly asking, "Is she in our district?"

I looked at him and shrugged my shoulders. After no one answered, she took off her cap and went into her stripping routine shedding most of her clothes.

Realizing it was probably me who arranged it, Gene just shook his head and laughed.

Out of the all previous commanders I had in the 15th, he seemed to be the one most interested in closer ties between the community and the police department. After leaving some of the community meetings we attended together, we discussed ways to accomplish it. Together we came up with the idea of opening a mini-police-station in the lower end. After discussing it with the business community, they found the idea acceptable.

There were a few vacant stores on the avenue from businesses fleeing the area, and I knew several owners of the stores that were empty. I solicited the owner of a vacant store on the Southeast corner of Frankford and Sellers Street, and rather than have the building fall victim to vandalism being unoccupied, he agreed to allow us the use of the first floor.

With the financial assistance from the Savings and Loan and other businesses, I was able to secure building materials to accomplish it.

Within the month, with the help of another person in 5 Squad and a few of the local kids, the doors were opened with a small ceremony.

Gene had two people assigned during the day-work shift and two assigned the 4 p.m. to midnight shift. It helped as far as the locals being able to have direct access to the police department closer to their neighborhood, rather than having to travel the distance to the district.

Gene and I became great friends while he was the captain of the district. When he was reassigned to another district in Southwest Philadelphia, he asked if I wanted to be transferred with him. The new district was quite a bit further from my home, but the truth in the matter, I already knew the lower end of the 15th and didn't want the hassle of learning a new district.

He was disappointed with my answer but I think he suspected it. We remained in contact with one another after he was reassigned to the other district, and we met several times for lunch. After he made inspector, he took over the Major Crimes Unit that was headquartered at the time in the old Frankford Arsenal Complex. I visited him there several times also, and we had a few laughs while reminiscing the past.

There were several changes of command with lieutenants and sergeants in other squads, but they had little to do with 5 Squad. There was one occasion where a Sergeant was about to reassign me to a patrol car for a lack of personnel, but the Corporal showed him a directive from the captain. It stated no one was to change 5 Squad personnel without the captain's approval. Indignant over the memo, he overrode the directive, and assigned me to a patrol car. Several hours later, I was recalled to the district and reassigned my foot-beat. I discovered later by the Corporal, when the captain found out I was reassigned without his permission, he reprimanded the sergeant for overriding his directive.

After that incident the sergeant's attitude toward me changed, as though it was something personal. I was happy to see him transferred after a short period of time. He also became a high-ranking member within the police department.

I always looked forward to when 2 Squad was on day-work. It gave me a chance to catch up on changes and current events in the squad. The sergeant of 5 Squad was new and he would stop and speak with me quite often. I remembered his father being in 2 Squad when I was first assigned to the district. Like several other policemen who were currently in the 15th, I remember their fathers being patrolmen as well.

For several days, I was hearing from a few people who live in the project about Leroy Williamson having a little bit of a mental problem. There was really nothing anyone could do without commitment papers, and my advice was to try and steer clear of him.

One summer day shortly thereafter around noon, I was speaking with the lieutenant from 2 Squad, when a call came out of a shooting and a hospital case in the 4700 block of Tackawanna Street. I quickly got in his car and we sped off to the scene. As we pulled into Tackawanna Street, we observed a man lying face down in the middle of the street. After turning him over, I realized he was obviously dead from observing several gunshot wounds to the chest. Several people came out of their project apartments as soon as we arrived, and told me the shooter was Leroy Williamson. After other officers arrived, I told the lieutenant to drive around to an address on Hawthorne Street, where I knew Leroy was living at the home of his parents. After arriving at the residence, I informed the lieutenant of Leroy's size and temperament, and that he was a professional prizefighter.

After walking up the steps, I knocked at the front door. Leroy looked out of the small diamond shaped window to see who it was and I said, "Roy, open the door."

He did as I asked without hesitation and I asked if he had a gun. He pointed to the sofa where it was lying in plain sight and I asked him to step outside. The lieutenant put his handcuffs on him and with the thickness of Leroy's wrists, the handcuffs only closed to the second notch. Knowing he had recently been arrested for dealing drugs I asked, "Roy, is there any drugs in the house? I don't want your parents to get caught up in this thing."

He said there was some marijuana in an end table, so I retrieved it and flushed it down the toilet. After the wagon crew came, we put him inside and it pulled away. I was about to get in the lieutenant's car when he gave me a strange look.

I asked, "What's wrong?"

He replied, "When you said he was big, I thought you were talking about someone overweight. I had no idea he was big that way. If I had, I would have had my gun out."

I laughed as we drove away from the scene. Before we reached the Homicide Unit at 8th and Race Street, there were already several calls from prominent sports people concerned about him. When the case was scheduled for court, he pleaded guilty to the homicide and I never had to make a court appearance. He was sentenced to life in prison, but only served several years before being paroled.

CHAPTER 25

Commendations

I was never a true believer in commendations; I always thought our commendations came every two weeks in the pay-box. Aside from the commendation with the lieutenant for the arrest of Leroy Williamson for homicide, there were several others I couldn't refuse, and one was the purse-snatch Mean Gene and I made. The other was a bank holdup at Frankford and Unity Street Gene and I made together.

    It happened like this. He drove down to the beat during the Christmas shopping holiday season, and was speaking with me about an on-going investigation. While sitting in his vehicle discussing it, a call came out of a holdup alarm at the bank at Frankford and Unity Street. Hearing the broadcast, he sped away to the scene which was only several blocks away. As we approached the intersection, I pointed to two men running from the bank across Frankford Avenue, heading east on Unity Street. Being a small one-way street with only one parking lane, I asked him to let me out at the head of the block and told him to drive to the other end. The suspects, after looking at us, quickly got in a late model Chevy. As the driver of the getaway car attempted to pull out of the parking space, the car stalled and the three men quickly exited the vehicle. As I approached from one end of the block, the captain closed in on the other end. With guns drawn the suspects quickly gave up. I put the handcuffs on two of the suspects linking them together, and asked the captain for his to link the third person. After a police wagon arrived, we put the prisoners inside.

We retrieved the money from the car, which was around $10,000 dollars and walking back to the bank. I mentioned to the captain, "I'm glad we didn't have a shootout with those guys."

"Why? Don't you think I can shoot?" he replied.

"No, it's not that. Your gun isn't loaded."

After opening the cylinder, he looked at the empty weapon and said, "Oh shit! You're right."

There were other incidences where a commendation was warranted, but as I mentioned, they didn't impress me. I used to try to sign bank logs twice daily, but due to activity sometimes it wasn't always possible.

After so many years in the district, there weren't many people I didn't know who worked in the different businesses. Usually when I entered the building, there would be a greeting of some sort from one of the tellers, or another bank employee. This was more than the case when I entered the branch of a savings and loan. I had more contact with this particular branch, due to the side work I was doing for the institution.

One day as I was entering the bank to sign the log, it seemed to be unusually quiet between tellers and patrons. There were a few people standing at the counter where deposit slips are kept, but I noticed no one seemed to be writing and no one was moving toward a teller for a transaction. As I went to the desk where the log was kept for my signature, there wasn't the usual greeting. I noticed a male standing by the rear door that faces the parking lot, and another I passed coming into the building.

It didn't take long to understand I walked in on a holdup in progress. Not wanting to alarm the holdup men and have someone accidently injured, I made my exit through the front door and continued down the street as though I hadn't realized what was taking place.

Two stores later, I stepped into the entry and notified police radio of what was happening. I asked for police cars to cover the parking lot in the rear, and as soon as a backup came to the front of the bank, we re-entered.

I grabbed who I believed was the lookout by the front door, as he tried to exit, and threw him down on the floor with my weapon at his head. The person in front of the teller being held up tried to make his exit along with the lookout at the rear door, but by that time, police had surrounded the getaway car in the parking lot.

After the apprehensions, the bank was abuzz with conversation from the employees as well as the patrons of how well the police handled the situation.

There was another memorable incident at the same bank when a local walked in with a briefcase and announced there was a bomb inside. When the call came out I was in the next block and quickly headed for the bank.

Through the front window, I observed Curtis Williamson, a brother to the boxer I arrested for murder. I knew he was known for dramatics of this sort, and after entering the bank, the assistant manager alerted me to the situation. For the safety of the bank personnel, he had already directed them to exit the rear door to the parking lot. Police had begun to arrive and as they entered the bank, I informed the lieutenant of the mental problems the person had.

Talking with the subject, I asked if there was a bomb inside. After putting on his crazy act, he told me there wasn't. I told him to open the case and empty it, and just as I figured, there were only papers inside. It's all part of having worked the same area for years.

At Frankford High School dismissal, I always tried to be there to walk along with the kids who took the El to different parts of the city. The school was only three blocks off the beat, but by doing it, it usually deterred any fights from breaking out. There were also a few stores and a newspaper stand in that route I didn't want to fall victim to theft.

One day as I was walking along with the kids, the owner of a sandwich shop alerted me to the fact the corner antique store still had the closed sign showing. She further stated the couple usually ordered sandwiches for lunch and hadn't come in that day. I knew the couple to be old, probably in their mid-seventies, from stopping in periodically to speak with them. Although they classified the store as an antique shop, it was more or less old things, and a means for the couple to earn a few dollars. After trying the door, I peered in and couldn't see anything unusual, so I told her I would look in on them after I cleared the Elevated Train stop.

Fifteen minutes later, I returned. After trying the door again without success, I went to the rear of the store to try to gain entry. Trying the rear door, to my surprise it opened. I took a few steps into the room and to my shock; I saw what appeared to be bloody hand marks and smears on the wall.

A little further into the backroom, the marks were more pronounced, and a pool of blood covered most of the floor. I immediately realized what I was seeing was only going to be the beginning of an investigation, and a few steps further into the room verified that thought. I saw the couple lying on the floor face up with a Ball-peen Hammer next to the bodies, and their heads seemed to be the source of the bloody mess. Noting the blood-stained hand marks and smears on the walls, it indicated to me the couple put up a hard fight with whoever the attacker or attackers were before being overcome.

Walking out into the store, I looked behind the counter and noticed the cash register open. There was no money in it, so I presumed they were victims of a robbery and thought, *"Even if they were robbed, there was no reason for this kind of brutality. They were two old defenseless people."*

After calling for a supervisor, I waited until he arrived. I put in a call to Northeast Detectives and the Homicide Unit, and after they arrived, I told them what I knew. Since it was the end of the day, a sector car came to guard the scene and I went to headquarters to fill out the necessary paperwork.

I don't know how the arrest was made, but the attacker turned out to be a fifteen-year-old boy. He had been released from a presumed robbery and beating death of an elderly shoemaker he was extorting money from in the Kensington section of the city.

CHAPTER 26

Regrets

I obviously don't regret situations and circumstances I had to deal with. Those are the facts. Some of the police command seemed less than enthusiastic when it came to the reality of a situation. Nothing points that out better than an incident I encountered around two years before I retired.

As I mentioned several times, the neighborhood was on a steady downhill decline for several years. Around 1986, there were a few women murdered in the late night hours, and that brought some unwanted attention to the area. The news articles seemed to be focusing on making it another Jack the Ripper type incident, rather than the picture as a whole.

One day, I was at the far end of the beat when a young man approached me. He identified himself as a reporter for the newspaper and wanted to do an interview about the Frankford area. I asked why he chose me and his reply was, "The corporal in the district said you were probably the most knowledgeable policeman about the Frankford area." After some words to that effect I was flattered, I agreed to give him the interview and we started walking north to the other end of the beat.

Amongst the questions he asked were questions about the recent homicides. I told him I was doing all I could do to help with the investigation, but at this point, I had no definitive answers. His conversation began to focus on how the neighborhood changed so dramatically in the last 15 years.

As we were walking, I stopped his conversation and pointed to a store that was boarded-up and said, "That used to be a store that sold work clothes."

He looked at me bewildered for a moment, wondering as to why I made that statement, but kept pressing me for knowledge about the district.

In the next block, I interrupted his questions again, pointing to another store and said, "That store that sells sneakers. That used to be a store that sold work clothes and work shoes."

Again, he looked in the direction of the store and seemed temporarily confused, but went right back to asking questions about the neighborhood's decline.

When we got to Margaret Street, the center of my beat, I pointed to a building on the Northeast Corner and said, "That Bingo hall was one of the largest work clothing stores in the city."

He replied, "That's the third time you interrupted our conversation to tell me about stores that used to sell work clothes. What's your point?"

"My point is, without a job you don't need work clothing. That's why they're no longer there."

I continued the conversation by naming the many manufacturing jobs that left the area, and how it turned a viable working class neighborhood into what it had become. I went on to name people and circumstances, who, through no fault on their own, became victims to unemployment when industry moved away.

After a little more conversation, he thanked me for the interview, and my insight of the neighborhood then walked away.

Within the hour, I received a radio call to go to the district. When I arrived the corporal told me to go upstairs and see the Divisional Inspector. After knocking at the door, I was admitted by his aid. Sitting behind his desk he looked up and said bluntly, "Who gave you permission to give an interview to a reporter?"

"No one Inspector, I didn't know I needed to get permission."

"Well you do. It's not your job to talk about why a neighborhood becomes distressed. Luckily, the reporter came back before he took the story to the newspaper office. I was able to squash it. No more interviews, Okay?"

"No problem," I replied.

This was the same inspector who also asked me to build a brick patio for his mother on city time.

After leaving the inspector's office, I realized I came one step closer to retirement.

Epilogue

The biggest injustice of that sentiment is to the people left behind. People I befriended while working in the district like Harry the window washer, a lifelong resident of Frankford, whose family history dated back over a hundred and fifty years. Several times a week, I would see him washing the front windows of the different stores on the avenue. He was by in large a local alcoholic, but through the years he had gained the respect of the merchants. Shortly before I retired, I found him dead on a platform of a building that was previously the neighborhood post office.

People like blind Teddy who had the newsstand at Frankford and Margaret Street for thirty years. Teddy was a big man who everyone knew and liked. When someone walked up to his newsstand and gave him a greeting, he would respond likewise by the sound of their voice. He had owned the newsstand long enough to tell the exact change deposited in the open cigar-box by the sound of the coin.

People like Lynwood, who never learned to write his name and signed his paycheck with an X. When a new teller at the bank wouldn't cash a check for lack of identification purposes, he would look me up to verify who he was, and on occasion I would cosign his paycheck.

People like Pauline Wilson, who wasn't a merchant, but a lively figure in the fact she always had something funny to say. She was a large dark-skinned black woman you could hear before you could see. Her normal voice was at least seven octaves higher than necessary, and the level grew exponentially with a few drinks. She was always a little awkward when she drank, and a few times I had to get her transportation to the local hospital when she fell injuring herself. She once told me as I helped her to her feet after a fall, *"Randy, you know what? I see you every day walking your beat like you be the cock of the walk. If I had the chance I'd f—k the hell out of you.... But baby, you just the wrong color."*

People like Benny Tucker and Roosevelt Brown: two guys who took their own time and money to organize the neighborhood football teams. At a community meeting I brought up that fact to a few influential people attending, and finally more than ten years after beginning the program, they were awarded a plaque from the city.

People like Bill Lamb who was a self appointed lifeguard at the city pool in the summer on his own time. He probably taught half the kids in that neighborhood how to swim. Every time we saw each other while I was on the beat he would yell out, "Hey Randy!" and accompany it with a hearty wave.

The Lu Family who ran the Chinese Restaurant. When a patron got out of hand one day and shoved Mrs. Lu, I responded to the radio call. Escorting the patron outside the restaurant, he kicked me. As the police wagon pulled up, the guy kicked me again. He was a big man and I grabbed him by the coat and ran his head into the closed backdoor of the police wagon. There happened to be one of three brothers who owned a men's clothing store across the street watching. After I put the offender in the wagon I heard someone yell, "Hey Randy look at this." I looked in his direction as he held up a cardboard sign with a number 10 on it.

I remembered the first day I met Victor and his two brothers. I was walking the beat one day in early spring and was approached by them.

After some conversation about the security of the business district and a few other incidentals, they asked my opinion about opening a man's clothing store. The few that were there that sold suits moved away for one reason or another, and that left only one store whose primary business was selling blue jeans. After showing them one of the vacant stores close to the intersection of Margaret Street, they thanked me and walked away.

Several weeks later, I saw them again when they were setting up their store. Fashions were changing from the traditional conservative style, to a little more flashy-trend, and looking at the stock they were putting on display, I realized they would probably do very well. Before I retired, they had expanded their business to three stores in different sections of the city.

While walking the beat, I would go in on occasion to fill out my patrol log, and indulge in general conversations with them and their salesman. We became very friendly and like the rest of the store owners, I listened to any complaints they might have.

During Christmas week, our hours were adjusted to cover the store hours on the avenue from 10 a.m. to 6 p.m. Holidays were always pretty busy; and the chance of a holdup or shoplifter was greater during those hours. At times looking into the store as I past, everyone seemed to be busy with customers buying clothing. During that week, I always stayed on the beat and waited until they cleared the register at 6 p.m. After they finished counting the money, I escorted one of the brothers to the night deposit box at the bank, and after the deposit, I would head to the district.

I grew to like them and their salesman for some of their words of wisdom. Barry Jackson one of the salesman and probably the most successful, would always pass a comment during the holiday shopping season, "Hey Randy, all I need is a little dustin' of snow. Just a little dustin', to make my holiday spirit brighter." He was of course right; it always seemed to put people in a better spending mode.

When they found out from other merchants I was doing work for their stores, they solicited me to do theirs as well.

There was one thing I thought was an ingenious idea for increasing business during the Christmas holiday shopping on the avenue. There were loudspeakers donated by a local music store that would play holiday music under the El. There was one song that was brilliantly placed and played about every 30 minutes. It was a recording of Jingle Bells sung by dog barks. As the beginning of the song: Ruff, Ruff, Ruff – Ruff, Ruff, Ruff, was heard, it seemed to drive the shoppers into the different stores to avoid laughing.

As my business flourished, I knew I had to make a decision, and that decision was whether to stay on the department, or hang it up. In August of 1989, I decided it was time to go, but in a way, it was like I never left the beat. I still had store owners requiring my work, and every time I was doing work at one of the stores on the avenue, there were always people stopping to say hello.

Several years after I retired, I received a disturbing phone call at home late on a Saturday afternoon. One of the neighborhood people I had known from the time he was a kid, called to tell me there was something unusual going on at the brothers' clothing store; there seemed to be a lot of police activity there.

He further stated there was an ambulance on the scene and someone mentioned one of the brothers being shot during an attempted holdup. Knowing my personal connection with the brothers, he felt I'd be interested. He was right of course, and I quickly drove to the scene. The police had already left, but speaking with Barry the salesman, I discovered not only one brother was shot, but two were shot. One was pronounced dead at the scene and the other died en route to the hospital.

I spoke briefly to Victor, the surviving brother who happened to be closing the store, and asked if I could do anything to help. For obvious reasons, my comment seemed to go unnoticed and I knew better than to ask about the incident.

After he locked the door and drove away, Barry filled me in on what took place. I knew the brothers carried firearms in the store during open hours, but it just so happened they were in the process of closing, and just put the cash for the day in the safe, and the pistols in a drawer behind the counter.

As the youngest brother was about to lock the door, the two holdup men forced their way in. After some words between them, one of the holdup men realized the brother behind the counter tripped the alarm. He fired a shot that struck him in the neck severing the aorta artery. The other brother coming to his aid was shot once in the chest and the bullet severed the main artery going into the heart. After hearing the news, my heart sunk with sadness.

The crowd of people that began to gather outside the store from the neighborhood, were just as shocked as I was to hear what happened. The brothers were well liked, and took an active part in the business association, and neighborhood in general. Some of his salesman, were people he hired as juniors and seniors while in Frankford High School, and in doing so, more than likely helped in giving them the incentive to go further in life.

After some conversation about different experiences we shared with the brothers, we parted. On the drive home I thought about how horrendous the incident was. Two great people killed over $125.

Several days later, I attended their double funeral on North Broad Street, and there was standing room only inside. Outside, there had to be a thousand people waiting to view the bodies. The showing of that many people was a testimonial to their popularity.

I'd also like to mention the many kids I watched grow up over the years. From little kids jumping around under the spray of a fire hydrant on a hot summer day; into mature responsible adults. Some of those relationships still exist to this day.

There had been many interesting incidents, far too many to catalogue in this book.

I could go on and on about the people I missed by leaving the department, but I feel it was the right decision at the right time. In retrospect, I don't know whether not taking the exams to go further up the ladder of promotions was an injustice to my family. I often wondered; *if I did, would I have had the knowledge that allowed me to be as effective in police work?*

On a personal note, I was lucky to have been assigned the 15th District. I've always been interested in the history of Philadelphia, and the Frankford section just teemed with it. Unfortunately, with the neighborhood's demise, I witnessed several homes demolished from the late 18th Century by people who purchased them, not realizing their historical significance. From the Dutch people who first settled the land, to the Quakers that followed, there's a rich history. The Frankford Friends Meeting House established in 1684 still stands at 4371 Waln Street, as well as the John Ruan House in the 4200 block of Griscom Street. The Ruan home was constructed in 1796 and was used as a hospital for recuperating Union soldiers during the Civil War. It's now a museum.

Frankford Historical Society located in the 1500 block of Orthodox Street, is a central bank of the history of the area too, and anyone interested in its history should begin at that point. Before you begin though, I would strongly advise looking at the Wikipedia website of Frankford. It gives a pretty good description of its past, and unfortunately its current conditions.

OTHER WORKS BY THIS AUTHOR ARE AS FOLLOWS:

Crossing the Blue Line:

A murder mystery of a female police officer found dead, in a small bathroom of a police district.

Veronica:

A serial killing type murder mystery, that takes place on Long Beach Island, N.J.

New Hope:

A Murder mystery that takes place in a live Theatre in New Hope, Penna.

Mystery of the Windowed Closet:

A paranormal filled with spirits and séances.

Mist in the Blue Bottle:

The sequel to Mystery of the Windowed Closet. A mystical Blue Bottle with the power beyond the psychics ability to control.

The Adventures of Mark and David:

A preteen adventure book that adult readers seemingly enjoy.

Biloxi:

An extensive novel set in the Antebellum South between 1850 and 1865. The story is set with the oncoming Civil War, running the blockade of southern ports, a sugar plantation in Cuba, and a host of other venues. Life, love, political corruption, human interaction, and tragedy, are all a part of this novel.